THE MIRACLES OF JESUS THE MESSIAH

THE MIRACLES OF JESUS THE MESSIAH

E. KEITH HOWICK

BOOKCRAFT
Salt Lake City, Utah

Library of Congress Catalog Card Number: 85-72871
ISBN 0-88494-540-5

First Printing, 1985

Printed in the United States of America

To Gail and Jodi

Key to Abbreviations

Abbreviation	Name of Work
	Scriptural references to the standard works of The Church of Jesus Christ of Latter-day Saints are abbreviated in the standard, self-identifying manner.
DNTC	Bruce R. McConkie, *Doctrinal New Testament Commentary*, vol. 1, *The Gospels* (Salt Lake City: Bookcraft, 1975).
Ed	Alfred Edersheim, *The Life and Times of Jesus the Messiah*, reprint ed. (Grand Rapids, Michigan: Wm. B. Eerdmans Publishing Company, 1981).
Ed (Temple)	Alfred Edersheim, *The Temple: Its Ministry and Services As They Were at the Time of Jesus Christ*, reprint ed. (Grand Rapids, Michigan: Wm. B. Eerdmans Publishing Company, 1982).
Farrar	Frederick W. Farrar, *The Life of Christ*, 2 vols. (New York: E. P. Dutton and Company, 1874).
FPM	Spencer W. Kimball, *Faith Precedes the Miracle* (Salt Lake City: Deseret Book Company, 1972).
Geikie	Cunningham Geikie, *The Life and Words of Christ*, revised ed., 2 vols. (New York: D. Appleton and Company, 1891, 1894).
HC	Joseph Smith, Jr., *History of The Church of Jesus Christ of Latter-day Saints*, ed. B. H. Roberts, 7 vols. (Salt Lake City: The Church of Jesus Christ of Latter-day Saints, 1949).
JC	James E. Talmage, *Jesus the Christ* (Salt Lake City: Deseret Book Company, 1959).

Josephus	*Josephus, Complete Works,* trans. Wm. Whiston (Grand Rapids, Michigan: Kregel Publications, 1971).
MD	Bruce R. McConkie, *Mormon Doctrine,* 2d ed. (Salt Lake City: Bookcraft, 1966).
MF	Spencer W. Kimball, *The Miracle of Forgiveness* (Salt Lake City: Bookcraft, 1969).
MM	Bruce R. McConkie, *The Mortal Messiah,* 4 vols. (Salt Lake City: Deseret Book Company, 1979–81).
Strauss	David Friedrich Strauss, *The Life of Jesus, Critically Examined,* trans. George Eliot (Messrs. George Allen and Company Ltd., n.p., 1906).
TG	*Topical Guide* (Salt Lake City: The Church of Jesus Christ of Latter-day Saints, 1979).
Trench	Richard Chenevix Trench, *Notes on the Miracles of Our Lord* (Westwood, New Jersey: Fleming H. Revell Company, n.d.).

Contents

Introduction

The standard King James Version of the Bible is used as the scriptural basis for each miracle discussed in this book. The Gospels of Matthew, Mark, Luke, and John record the miracles, but the following important facts need to be considered when studying them.

First, not every miracle that Jesus performed during his ministry is recorded. In fact, from the examination of the scriptures (see chapter 1), it is evident that the Gospel writers were extremely selective in the miracles they chose to record.

Second, while several miracles are exclusive to one Gospel and others appear in two or more, only one miracle is found in all four Gospels. Where miracles are found in more than one Gospel, the writers do not always agree on the order of the miracles, the circumstances surrounding them, nor their descriptive detail. I have not attempted to reconcile these discrepancies and disagreements except in limited instances where the interpretations and circumstances appear to warrant it.

Third, discrepancies in scripture should not discredit its authenticity; each narrative is unique, and each writer was obviously selective. There are problems involving translation, language variance, and ancient additions and deletions. Also, familiarity with a given miracle may have led the Gospel writers to eliminate circumstances they felt were self-explanatory.[1] Finally, an obvious problem is that different men see things differently, even when witnessing the same event. However, these differences in the accounts only serve to confirm the individuality and authenticity of the Gospels.

Matthew and John were Apostles—eyewitnesses to all that Jesus did during his ministry. Matthew recorded many of the miracles in a straightforward, factual manner that rarely emphasized detail. Most of the miracles John recorded were not referred to in the other Gospels, so apparently he attempted to fill in the gaps left by the others.

Mark appears to be the true "reporter," usually including more explicit detail than the other writers. Most scholars feel that he did not witness the events he wrote of, but presumably received his information from Peter.[2]

Finally, Luke seems to be a mixture. He was an early disciple and thus gained much of his information firsthand; but in addition he was a compiler of the biblical record, reporting material gleaned from other witnesses.

The Gospels of Matthew, Mark, and Luke are commonly called the synoptic Gospels, meaning that these writers used a similar approach in presenting the events of Jesus' life. (John, as noted earlier, often reported events unrecorded in the other Gospels, and he wrote in a different style.) Throughout this book there are frequent references to these first three Gospels as the Synoptics, or the synoptic Gospels.

Thirty-seven specific miracles are discussed in this book.[3] The names of the miracles are assigned on the basis of the circumstances surrounding them. Thirty-four of the miracles are readily recognized. The remaining three consist of what I have named the Multitude of Miracles, Passing Unseen (Before the Resurrection), and Passing Unseen (After the Resurrection).

I have presented my discussion of Christ's miracles topically rather than sequentially or chronologically. It is obviously difficult to state with complete assurance the exact meaning that Jesus intended for each of his miracles, actions, parables, discourses, and words. However, I feel that the Gospel writers selected these miracles from the thousands they witnessed (or otherwise learned of) in an attempt to better illustrate the principles Jesus taught. Through careful consideration of the scriptures describing the miracles, the scriptural circumstances surrounding them, other scriptural support and evidence, the historical evaluation of the times, the recorded Jewish expectations of the Messiah, and some of the foremost authoritative and knowledgable writers, I have attempted to determine the principal teachings intended by the Gospel writers.

The body of the book is divided into eight parts and nineteen chapters. Chapter 1 deals with the topic of miracles in general and includes a discussion on the Multitude of Miracles. Chapters 2 through 18 examine specific miracles as they are recorded in the Gospels. Chapter 19 deals with the general message of the miracles. The discussion of each miracle begins with a passage quoted from the relevant scriptural text. If the miracle appears in more than one Gospel, the account is drawn from the Gospel that reports the miracle most clearly. (Cross-references to the other scriptural accounts are listed by chapter and verse only.) When a passage of the quoted scriptural text is used in the discussion, no footnote appears (the whole source having been referred to at the beginning of the discussion). The same is true of the cross-references quoted. Some additional cross-references may also appear, such as changes made by the Joseph Smith Translation of the Bible (herein referred to as JST).[4]

Those sacred occurrences referred to as "miracles" were just that—miracles! The narrators who recorded them were great men, originally of ordinary stature, but moved upon by the Holy Spirit to write and preserve the record for all. The miracles of Jesus stand on their own in association with his teachings: the miracles testify of the authenticity of the doctrine, and the doctrine teaches the necessity of the miracles. "To the believer in the divinity of Christ, the miracles are sufficiently attested; to the unbeliever they appear but as myths and fables."[5]

One particular scriptural passage is most important when considering the following material. It was spoken by the Lord and recorded by John, the Apostle "whom Jesus loved" (John 21:7, 20): "Search the scriptures; for in them ye think ye have eternal life: and they are they which testify of me" (John 5:39).

Part One

The Miracles
in Perspective

Miracles   1

Historical Expectations, the Miracles, and Jesus

The miracle is a most extraordinary thing. It appears to run counter to life's experience and facts. Yet within sacred scripture, the miracle is seemingly a daily occurrence. One cannot read the Bible, either the Old or the New Testament, without encountering miracle upon miracle. Moses, for example, led the rebellious and unbelieving Israelites from day to day by miracles, and those people were held in wondering awe of God, for Israel's God was a God of miracles.

In Pharaoh's court, at the direction of Moses, Aaron cast down his rod and it became a serpent. Pharaoh immediately called upon his magicians and they did likewise. Aaron's rod then swallowed up the rods of the magicians (see Exodus 7:10—12). Thus began the great exhibition of signs and wonders to persuade Pharaoh to let enslaved Israel go.

The magicians continued to duplicate the signs and wonders that God had given Moses. They also turned water to blood (see Exodus 7:19—22) and brought the plague of frogs (see Exodus 8:5—7) upon the land of Egypt. But thereafter, the magicians could no longer duplicate the miraculous plagues of lice and flies, cattle disease, boils, hail, locusts, and finally the death of the firstborn; and they were forced to admit, "This is the finger of God" (Exodus 8:19).

This was the beginning of the miraculous events that became Israel's heritage. Miracles had occurred prior to Moses' time, but Moses was the great wonder-worker. By the power of God he parted the Red Sea and delivered the Israelites from the oppressive hands of their enemies. The Lord fed them manna from heaven for forty years in the wilderness, and even their "raiment waxed not old upon [them], . . . these forty years" (Deuteronomy 8:4). To this richness was added Elijah and Elisha, other prophets, and the traditions and writings of the Rabbis.

> From this point of view, the whole Old Testament becomes the perspective in which the figure of the Messiah stands out. And perhaps the most valuable element in Rabbinic commentation on Messianic times is that in which, as so frequently, it is explained that all the miracles and deliverances of Israel's past would be re-enacted, only in a much wider manner, in the days of the Messiah. Thus the whole past was symbolic, and typical of the future—the Old Testament the glass, through which the universal blessings [of the Messianic days] were seen.[1]

All this was a prelude to the miracles of the Master and Messiah. He came to a people whose tradition was full of miracles. Given this heritage the Jews could believe in the miracles of Jesus, and in fact many did, even though they did not accept him as the Messiah. Their Messiah was to be a second Moses, and yet greater, the greatest of the prophets.[2] They expected him to perform miracles.[3] John confirms this, declaring the people's reaction: "When Christ cometh, will he do more miracles than these which this man [Jesus] hath done?" (John 7:31).

Not only was the Messiah expected to perform miracles, but the very miracles that he was to perform were anticipated. The Lord, through Moses, fed the children of Israel in the wilderness (see Exodus 16:14—17); should not Christ do likewise?[4] The reaction of the people testified that they remembered and understood when he did (see chapter 2). He was to open the eyes of the blind (see Isaiah 42:7) and raise the dead (see 1 Kings 17; 2 Kings 4), for he could do no less than the greatest of his ancient prophets. Of the Messiah, Isaiah had prophesied: "Then the eyes of the blind shall be opened, and the ears of the deaf shall be unstopped. Then shall the lame man leap as an hart, and the tongue of the dumb sing!" (Isaiah 35:5—6.)

The people of Christ's time looked for these scriptural prophecies to be literally fulfilled. The New Testament writers understood that in Christ the prophecies had been fulfilled, and so recorded it. It is no wonder they write plainly that Christ caused the blind to see and unstopped the ears of the deaf. In giving speech to the dumb and successfully commanding the lame, the palsied, and the paralytic to take up their beds and walk, he was literally fulfilling that which was expected of the looked-for Messiah.[5]

Why then were these very happenings questioned by the Jews? The answer lies not in their disbelief in the miracles, but in Jesus—so they accused him of performing miracles through the power of the prince of devils, Beelzebub. Their question was not, "Was a miracle performed?" The public occurrences of his miracles made asking this question impossible. Instead, their question was, "By what power or in what name do you perform miracles?" They did not question his ability, but his authority. They recognized the claim to the Messiahship and demanded, "Show us a sign." But they wanted more than the signs that merely fulfilled the prophecies of miracles, for Jesus more than satisfied those expectations. They desired of him a specific sign from heaven, the Messianic sign of the Son of Man. They did not look for the meek, loving, kind, and all-merciful man who had been raised in Nazareth as a carpenter, whose mother, father, brothers, and sisters they knew. It was the political Messiah the Jews looked for—and still do.

The Messiah was to rid Israel of the yoke of bondage, as Moses had done; to restore their former glory and honor among nations, as David had done; to come with power to rid them forever of all their enemies; and to call down God's vengeance on those that had despitefully used them. The Jews believed in miracles, even the miracles of Jesus; but they would not believe Jesus was the Messiah. They looked for and sought from him the sign of his second coming, while the signs he gave them were of his first coming. They looked beyond the mark, and missed him.

The Purpose of Miracles

Miracles are signs. The scriptural writers at times describe them as "wonders," "powers," and "signs" (see Matthew 9:6; 24:24; Acts 14:3; Romans 15:19; Hebrews 2:4).

In the Old Testament, signs emanated from God for many reasons. For example, they verified God's word, as in the sundial of Hezekiah (see 2 Kings 20:4—11); confirmed God's direction, as in the fleece of Gideon (see Judges 6:36—40); or confirmed God's call, as with the mantle of Elijah as it fell from him to Elisha (see 2 Kings 2:13—14).

The miracles of Jesus in the New Testament were also signs. Each miracle had its use and meaning within Jesus' ministry, generally falling into one or more of the following categories: to witness his identity as the Messiah; to witness his authority and power; to evidence and confirm his teachings; and to express his compassion.

To witness his identity as the Messiah. The miracles were Jesus' credentials, presented to the people in general and the leaders in particular as signs of his divinity. These signs enforced Jesus' claim to the Messiahship, further revealed his character, and expanded the evidence of his divine mission. In this context some miracles were directed specifically to the people, some to the leaders of the Jews, some to the Law, and some to the Apostles. All this that they might prove, attest, and verify that Jesus was the Christ, the expected Messiah.

To witness his authority and power. The discussion on "The Multitude of Miracles" will readily attest that both the ordinary people and the leaders of the Jews recognized that Christ held the power to perform miracles. Yet they often questioned his authority. Certain miracles required all who witnessed and heard of them to decide concerning Christ, and thereby to believe or disbelieve, to accept or reject him and his claim to divine authority. These miracles attested to his power over all things—the laws of nature, the elements, life, death, bodily affliction of any kind, and the world of evil spirits.

To evidence and confirm his teachings. Miraculous signs brought Jesus attention early in his ministry. With every miracle more of the curious followed and the believers looked on with awe. These miracles were intended to open the hearts of both those who witnessed and those who received them. To supplement and enhance them, in every instance the miracles were followed by instruction. Faith and belief in Christ often resulted. Although this belief was born of signs and miracles rather than a deep-seated knowledge of Jesus' divinity, it fostered faith that brought many to the Messiah. Through miracles Christ taught proper judgment, correct use of his power, testimony of the Father, and more. These miracles illustrated his sacred truths, and convinced or encouraged others to rely on him and to actively seek his blessings.

To express his compassion. In the Sermon on the Mount and at other times, Jesus detailed the divine relationship that was to exist among those who followed him. "Do unto others"; "love your enemies"; "bless them that curse you"; "turn the other cheek"; "go the extra mile"; "forgive men their trespasses"; "judge not"; "freely ye have received, freely give"—Jesus exemplified these principles in his miracles as in no other recorded instances. The miracles demonstrated the compassion that he taught in his sermons and parables. They were deeds of mercy that relieved human suffering. Even when he sought privacy and seclusion so that he might rest, suffering people sought him out and he healed them. In this, Matthew noted, he fulfilled Isaiah's prophecy, for he "took our infirmities, and bare our sicknesses" (Matthew 8:17; see Isaiah 53:4).

The Lord's teachings were evidenced and exemplified by miracles, giving richness and power to his truths. Those truths were at times obscured from the spiritually diseased, their true meaning being enmeshed in current events, in the future, and in the Messiah himself.

Miracles are a part of the gospel. Signs follow those who believe. They benefit recipient and witness alike, both physically and spiritually, and testify to the truth and divinity of the Lord and his work.

Natural Laws, the Laws of God, and Miracles

Do miracles contradict natural laws? Are they a part of such laws? Are miracles an extension of them? Do any laws govern the working of miracles? These questions have caused speculation for centuries. Unnumbered volumes could not satisfactorily resolve the divergence of opinion on this matter. But man's desire to bind God to natural laws has little or no meaning unless man's inter-pretation of those laws includes the existence of their author.[6] One truth seems self-evident: regardless of man's arguments or theories, some laws are outside his limited understanding and experience, and they are beyond his power to control or mimic.

Nature contains many wonderful miracles, and perhaps the miracles of Jesus do not manifest God's power any more than ordinary and often-repeated natural processes. But his miracles are a different manifestation. For example, man may plant a seed or seedling; it will grow and develop, using the soil, moisture, and the sun. Each year the resulting vine uses those natural ele-ments to produce grapes that man nurtures and processes into wine. This surely is a natural miracle, but it is quite different from drawing the best wine from pots filled with water, and doing it without so much as a command.

Some attempt to ascribe laws to the miracles, theorizing that they are the acceleration of natural processes; others assign names to unknown orders and keenly hope for the day when man can discover and duplicate the processes. But surely he who gave this earth its body of natural law can on occasion modify that law, place it in abeyance, or subject it to a higher law so that his designs and needs might be accomplished.

God speaks at all times and to all people through normal and everyday natural laws, laws that are a vast, unbroken attestation of him. The miracle, however, is beyond the ordinary operations of natural law, and reveals the very powers of God.[7]

The miracle, then, is not unnatural or in contravention of natural law at all, but is higher than natural law, at least as we know it. The natural law that we know is not lost in the miracle; it is merely suspended.

So what is a miracle? Consider the following thoughts:

Elder James E. Talmage: We arbitrarily classify as miracles only such phenomena as are unusual, special, transitory, and wrought by an agency beyond the power of man's control . . . , the operation of a power transcending our present human understanding. [8]

Elder Bruce R. McConkie: But in the gospel sense, miracles are those occurrences wrought by the power of God which are wholly beyond the power of man to perform. Produced by a supernatural power, they are marvels, wonders, and signs, which cannot be duplicated by man's present powers or by any powers which he can obtain by scientific advancements. Miracles in the gospel sense are gifts of the Spirit; they take place when the Lord on his own motion manifests his powers or when man by faith prevails upon Deity to perform supernatural events. [9]

Richard C. Trench: Miracles . . . are ultimate resources, reserved for the great needs of God's kingdom, not its everyday incidents; they are not cheap off-hand expedients, which may always be appealed to, but come only into play when nothing else would have supplied their room. [10]

What is a miracle? It is a gift from God to man to fulfill a need, either temporal or spiritual, that man cannot accomplish without God's divine hand. And once received and seen, it leaves man in reverence of that God who granted the divine gift.

The Multitude of Miracles

Matthew 4:23—24

23. And Jesus went about all Galilee, teaching in their synagogues, and preaching the gospel of the kingdom, and healing all manner of sickness and all manner of disease among the people.

24. And his fame went throughout all Syria: and they brought unto him all sick people that were taken with divers diseases and torments, and those which were possessed with devils, and those which were lunatick, and those that had the palsy; and he healed them.

Mark 1:32—34, 39

32. And at even, when the sun did set, they brought unto him all that were diseased, and them that were possessed with devils.

33. And all the city was gathered together at the door.

34. And he healed many that were sick of divers diseases, and cast out many devils; and suffered not the devils to speak, because they knew him.

39. And he preached in their synagogues throughout all Galilee, and cast out devils.

Mark 6:53—56

53. And when they had passed over, they came into the land of Gennesaret, and drew to the shore.

54. And when they were come out of the ship, straightway they knew him,

55. And ran through that whole region round about, and began to carry about in beds those that were sick, where they heard he was.

56. And whithersoever he entered, into villages, or cities, or country, they laid the sick in the streets, and besought him that they might touch if it were but the border of his garment: and as many as touched him were made whole.

Matthew 15:29—30

29. And Jesus departed from thence, and came nigh unto the sea of Galilee; and went up into a mountain, and sat down there.

30. And great multitudes came unto him, having with them those that were lame, blind, dumb, maimed, and many others, and cast them down at Jesus' feet; and he healed them.

Matthew 12:15—16

15. But when Jesus knew it, he withdrew himself from thence: and great multitudes followed him, and he healed them all;

16. And charged them that they should not make him known.

Matthew 14:14

14. And Jesus went forth, and saw a great multitude, and was moved with compassion toward them, and he healed their sick.

Matthew 9:35

35. And Jesus went about all the cities and villages, teaching in their synagogues, and preaching the gospel of the kingdom, and healing every sickness and every disease among the people.

Matthew 19:2

2. And great multitudes followed him; and he healed them there.

Luke 6:17—19

17. And he came down with them and stood in the plain, and the company of his disciples, and a great multitude of people out of all Judea and Jerusalem, and from the sea coast of Tyre and Sidon, which came to hear him, and to be healed of their diseases;

18. And they that were vexed with unclean spirits: and they were healed.

19. And the whole multitude sought to touch him: for there went virtue out of him, and healed them all.

Luke 7:19—22

19. And John calling unto him two of his disciples sent them to Jesus, saying, Art thou he that should come? or look we for another?

20. When the men were come unto him, they said, John Baptist hath sent us unto thee, saying, Art thou he that should come? or look we for another?

21. And in that same hour he cured many of their infirmities and plagues, and of evil spirits; and unto

many that were blind he gave sight.

22. Then Jesus answering said unto them, Go your way, and tell John what things ye have seen and heard; how that the blind see, the lame walk, the lepers are cleansed, the deaf hear, the dead are raised, to the poor the gospel is preached.

Mark 6:5

5. And he could there do no mighty work, save that he laid his hands upon a few sick folk, and healed them.

Cross-references:

Matthew 8:16—17   Matthew 14:34—36   Mark 3:10
Luke 4:40—41   Luke 9:11   JST Matthew 4:22

Generally, when one is asked to recall the miracles of Jesus, it comes to mind that he healed the blind, the lame, and the sick, and raised the dead. The tendency is to limit the number of miracles to the thirty-three or thirty-four specifically identified in the Gospels. The Multitude of Miracles is often overlooked because of the lack of detail with which the Gospel writers refer to them. But within this lack of detail lies the grandeur of these miracles. Twelve examples of the multitude of miracles follow.

Matthew 4:23—24. Matthew reports that Jesus was tempted in the wilderness, that John the Baptist had been cast into prison, and that Jesus had commenced his early travels preaching that the kingdom of heaven was at hand. After the call of Peter, Andrew, James, and John, Matthew records, Jesus was teaching in the synagogues of Galilee and "healing all manner of sickness and all manner of disease among the people." Although this is a very general statement, it is extremely revealing of the early ministry of Jesus. Far from being restrictive in his miracles, the Master was granting them to many. Continuing, Matthew states that Jesus' fame went throughout Syria, and that those suffering from divers diseases and torments, those possessed with devils, the mentally ill, and the palsied were brought to him. The scripture then testifies that he healed them all.

The marvel of this experience is that unlike the purposeful miracles directed to individuals that one generally thinks of, here Jesus was healing large hosts of people, though doubtless on an individual basis. The reaction of the people to all this seemed quite natural and honest. They came to him wanting to be healed and to have the people they loved healed. The miracles immediately drew the attention of the people to Jesus, and the message would have been heard as it was passed from person to person and from village to village—a healer was among them! Pleas from the sick to be taken to Jesus must have rent the air. They had received an opportunity to gain relief from their illnesses of the moment or of a lifetime . . . and "he healed them." Such healings are the greatest examples of the Savior's unlimited compassion in all of scripture.

Mark 1:32—34. Mark records that it was the Sabbath, and Jesus had been teaching in the synagogue at Capernaum. The people there were astonished at his doctrine and recognized that he spoke with authority. It was the custom at the time to teach from the existing rabbinical writings, promulgating only doctrine that could be supported by a recognized rabbinical authority. Instead, the Lord taught using himself as the authority, and it astounded and astonished his hearers. Jesus not only taught the people, but in the synagogue he attested to his power when he cast an unclean spirit out of one possessed.

From the synagogue, the Lord retired to the house where Peter's wife's mother lay sick. The Apostles entreated the Lord in her behalf, and he healed her. This was the second miracle performed on this Sabbath day. Since it was the Sabbath, the people could not travel; to carry the sick to Christ would have been forbidden. They could walk only two thousand paces, the maximum permitted length of a Sabbath journey under rabbinical law.[11] So they waited. So much excitement had been created by the Lord's miracles that when the final blast of the trumpet signaled that the Sabbath was over, and "when the sun did set," the people brought their diseased and possessed to him.

The sick came from every street in Capernaum until "all the city was gathered together at the door." There was no question in their minds but that Jesus would heal them. His characteristics, not detailed to us but undoubtedly known to the people, had endeared him to them. And they came to receive of his great compassion. So far as the record shows, he did not teach or preach to them. He had done that earlier. He just "healed many that were sick of divers diseases, and cast out many devils."

Mark 1:39. After the experience in Capernaum, Jesus departed to a solitary place. Peter and other disciples found him and reported that all men sought him. Jesus returned to his mission, preached in the synagogues throughout Galilee, and "cast out devils."

Is it any wonder that all men sought him? The healer of body and soul, who taught with authority and not as the scribes, was giving freely of his great compassion. From these few passages it is obvious that many, many miracles were performed.

Mark 6:53—56. Prior to Mark's recording this experience he records the miraculous feeding of the five thousand and the singular experience of Jesus walking on the water. Concluding this he notes that they landed on the shore in the land of Gennesaret. Jesus' fame had preceded him because of the many miracles he had already performed, and the scripture reports that the people "knew him." They ran about the whole region and told everyone that he was in their midst. They carried their sick to him, for they knew he would heal them. Through every city and village and in the countryside, the word of his coming preceded him. Wherever he went the people desired his compassion, laid their sick in the streets, and begged to merely touch the border of his garment; and as many as touched him were made whole.

Matthew 15:29—30. After Jesus had healed the Syrophenician woman's child, he went up to a mountain, one of his favorite places for teaching, and the people came to him. They brought the lame, the blind, the dumb, the maimed, and many others, and placed them at Jesus' feet, and he healed them. The people stayed with the Lord three days, being fed first by spiritual truths of the kingdom, and then by the physical nourishment of the miraculous meal of loaves and fishes. This multitude consisted of four thousand men, not counting women and children.

Matthew 12:15—16. Again it was a Sabbath day. Jesus healed a man's withered hand, after which multitudes followed him— and he healed them all.

Matthew 14:14. Here it reports that at the feeding of the five thousand (a count that again excluded women and children) the Savior healed all the sick in the multitude.

Matthew 9:35. This scripture records that Jesus healed every sickness and every disease among the people.

Matthew 19:2. In this instance Jesus again had multitudes follow him and he healed them.

Luke 6:17—19. After Jesus had prayed all night he called his Apostles. He then preached in the plain, and a multitude came down to hear him teach and to be healed of their diseases. Some of the group were vexed with unclean spirits, and he healed them. The people's emotions soared, and they sought to touch him. The Lord's compassion must have been boundless. Christ, the great healer, must have been touched deeply, for Luke reports that "virtue [went] out of him, and healed them all."

Luke 7:19—22. While imprisoned, John the Baptist sent two of his disciples to question Jesus, to ask if it was "he that should come," or if they should look for another. Jesus asked them to observe the miracles of healing he was performing and then report them to John. He then cured many people of their infirmities and plagues.

Mark 6:5. In his home town of Nazareth Jesus could do no mighty work because of the people's unbelief; although Mark records, almost nonchalantly, "save that he laid his hands upon a few sick folk, and healed them." There had been so many miracles that "a few sick folk" may have seemed hardly anything at all.

The impression gained in reading the Gospels is that Jesus healed thousands. The miracles were, by sheer number, overpowering. Everywhere Jesus went he healed the sick and diseased. He did not perform just thirty or forty spectacular miracles —his was a ministry of spectacular miracles. The detailed miracles were recorded for specific purposes by inspired writers. They were selected from the thousands of miracles to instruct, to confirm, and to complete the teachings of Christ.[12]

Miracles serve a unique purpose. They astound and instantly generate wonder and excitement. They jolt people from the doldrums of common existence, and summon them to open their eyes to a more spiritual plane. It was not evil to request a miracle, for most of the miracles recorded were requested to fill personal needs. The sin lies in the disbelief in the miracles, and the disbelief in him who grants them. The miracles were Christ's signs to gather the people as a hen gathers her chicks, to teach principles and doctrines, and to show compassion. And above all, they attested to his Messiahship.

Part Two

Jesus' Messiahship Witnessed to the People

A Remembrance of Old Testament Events

The Raising of the Widow's Son

Luke 7:11—17

11. And it came to pass the day after, that he went into a city called Nain; and many of his disciples went with him, and much people.

12. Now when he came nigh to the gate of the city, behold, there was a dead man carried out, the only son of his mother, and she was a widow: and much people of the city was with her.

13. And when the Lord saw her, he had compassion on her, and said unto her, Weep not.

14. And he came and touched the bier: and they that bare him stood still. And he said, Young man, I say unto thee, Arise.

15. And he that was dead sat up, and began to speak. And he delivered him to his mother.

16. And there came a fear on all: and they glorified God, saying, That a great prophet is risen up among us; and, That God hath visited his people.

17. And this rumour of him went forth throughout all Judea, and throughout all the region round about.

The Gospels record three instances of Jesus raising the dead. The first is that of the widow's son, recorded by Luke. All three synoptic gospels record the raising of the daughter of Jairus, and John records the raising of Lazarus.

Traditionally, the raising of the daughter of Jairus is discussed first, the raising of the widow's son second, and the raising of Lazarus last. Presumably, this traditional approach gives maximum emphasis to Christ's power over death, each body having been dead longer then the previous one. However, this sequence does not adequately explain the doctrinal teachings of these miracles; there is much more to be gleaned from the raisings than the Lord's obvious power over death.

The raising of the daughter of Jairus and the raising of Lazarus are discussed respectively in chapters 8 and 10 of this book. This chapter discusses the raising of the widow's son.

From the reading of the scripture it appears that the Lord had never encountered this widow before. The woman expresses no faith in or prior knowledge of Jesus. The meeting of the Savior and the widow was not miraculous, and appears to have happened in the normal and natural course of events. In other words, at first glance there appears to be no specific reason for this miracle. Perhaps this is the reason historical evaluators have assumed it to be merely a second evidence of the Lord's power over death and an example of his compassion. But this particular event did not just happen—the woman's son was not raised from the dead by accident. Here was not only an awakening of the dead young man, but also an awakening of a dead Israel to its Messiah.

Every Jewish household looked forward to the coming of the Messiah. Jewish life centered around religion, and this emphasis was taught in every home in Israel.[1] From their infancy Jewish children were taught the holy scriptures, and "it was, indeed, no idle boast that the Jews 'were from their swaddling-clothes . . . trained to recognize God as their Father, and as the Maker of the world;' that, 'having been taught the knowledge (of the laws) from earliest youth, they bore in their souls the image of the commandments;' . . . they were 'brought up in learning,' 'exercised in the laws,' 'and made acquainted with the acts of their predecessors in order to [sic] their imitation of them.' "[2]

These teachings and laws, "the acts of their predecessors," were indelibly imprinted upon every child's memory for one purpose—to prepare for the long-awaited Messiah. The whole of the Old Testament was nothing more than the perspective from which the Messiah would be measured and recognized. The great miracles of the Old Testament would have been recited in each home in anticipation of the coming Messiah, and the great deeds of the heroic prophets, such as Elijah and Elisha, would have been told and retold. "Thus the whole past was symbolic, and typical of the future—the Old Testament the glass, through which the universal blessings of [the Messianic] days were seen."[3] Israel expected the Messiah to perform the miracles of Israel's past.[4] Therefore, this Old Testament expectation was, in part, fulfilled by the raising of the widow's son.

Consider the following Old Testament experiences.

1 Kings 17:17–24. As the chapter begins, Elijah informs Ahab, the king, that no rain would fall upon the earth except at Elijah's word. The Lord then commanded Elijah to hide for his safety. In his hiding place a raven fed him morning and evening, and the brook Cherith gave him water to drink. However, with no rain upon the land to replenish the waters of the brook, it soon dried up. The Lord then instructed Elijah to go to Zarephath, where he had prepared a widow to sustain the prophet.

Elijah, the widow, and her son had survived for some time by eating miraculously replenished meal and oil, but the son of the widow fell sick and died. The widow became distraught and railed upon Elijah for the death of her only son. Elijah took the son to the loft and laid him on his bed. After crying to the Lord, Elijah "stretched himself upon the child three times" and again cried unto the Lord for the return of the child's spirit, whereupon "the Lord heard the voice of Elijah; and the soul of the child came into him again, and he revived." Elijah took the child down and "delivered him unto his mother," and the mother believed.

2 Kings 4:7–37. A similar experience involved Elisha, the successor to Elijah, and the Shunammite woman. The woman had often given refreshment to Elisha as he passed by her house on his travels. She recognized him to be a man of God, and she and her husband set up a room in their home so that Elisha,

should he desire, might stop and rest. Elisha asked the woman what he could do to repay her for this kindness. She desired a child, but feeling she was too old to have a child, she withheld her answer. Elisha's servant answered for the woman, and told Elisha that she had no children. Elisha promised her a son in her old age, and it was so. But when the son was grown, he was suddenly taken ill and died. The body was laid upon the bed held in readiness for Elisha, whom the woman then set out to find.

When she found Elisha she informed him of her son's death. Elisha sent a servant with his staff to lay it upon the child. This the servant did, but nothing happened. Then Elisha came and "lay upon the child, and put his mouth upon his mouth, and his eyes upon his eyes, and his hands upon his hands: and he stretched himself upon the child; and the flesh of the child waxed warm. Then he returned, and walked in the house to and fro; and went up, and stretched himself upon him: and the child sneezed seven times, and the child opened his eyes." Elisha called for the mother and told her to "take up thy son," and she fell at his feet in gratitude.

These exciting reports from the Old Testament would have been taught over and over in every Jewish household. Thus the raising of the widow's son became a reminder to Israel.

And now to the Savior's miracle.

It was the day after Jesus had taught in Capernaum and had healed the centurion's servant. He had walked to Nain, a city in the area.[5] With Jesus were many of the disciples and "much people." As the Lord approached the city gate, they encountered another multitude of people in a quite different procession.

Undoubtedly the Lord, as was his custom, had been teaching and discussing the kingdom of heaven along the way with those who followed him. Now they were approached by the most grievous of sorrows—the funeral procession for a loved one. A dead son was being carried out, "the only son of his mother, and she was a widow." The anxiety of such a tragedy (not only death, but the death of an only son) would have immediately aroused compassion in Jesus. He could envision the mother's future desolation and loneliness. The mourning of an only son was prescribed, symbolically following Old Testament restraints (see Jeremiah 6:26; Amos 8:10; Zechariah 12:10). Paid mourners would have punctuated the real grief of the mother and would have preceded the company. The procession would have included those with flutes, cymbals, and perhaps trumpets, along with genuinely mourning friends and relatives.[6] It was in this setting that the Lord of Life met the widow's pain and grief at her son's death.

The Lord, undoubtedly moved with compassion, voiced his request to "weep not." However, the circumstance of the miracle, rather than the woman's personal sorrow, provides the insight into the teaching invoked by the miracle. Here was a widow whose only son was dead, a circumstance similar to that involving the prophets Elijah and Elisha already noted. Would not this similarity stir memories and arouse expectations in those who were about to witness this great miracle? Heedless of standard ceremonial observances, Jesus moved to the funeral procession and touched the bier. He had made physical contact with the dead, the greatest of all Levitical defilements; and in his day, this was rabbinically equated with endless terrors.[7] Jesus then spoke. "Young man, I say unto thee, Arise. And he that was dead sat up, and began to speak. And he delivered him to his mother."

The expectation was fulfilled—the widow's only son was raised from the dead and returned once again to his mother. Yet there was more, for Jesus used no contortions nor staff, nor did he lay his hands upon the lifeless body. The young man's life was restored solely by Jesus' divine word, thereby showing Christ to be greater than the prophets of old.

No Jewish citizen, no descendant of Abraham, Isaac, and Jacob could have missed the association. The reactions of the people, first fear and then joyous praise, seem to confirm this. "They glorified God, saying, That a great prophet is risen up among us; and, That God hath visited his people." The Gospel writers later emphasized this obvious association when they recorded the Lord's question to the disciples, "Whom do men say that I the Son of man am? And they said [echoing the expressions of the people], Some say that thou art John the Baptist: some, Elias [Elijah]." (Matthew 16:13—14.) The connection was too clear to have been overlooked. He did not restrain those who had witnessed the miracle from tellings others, as he did on other occasions. Rather, he wanted them to tell others. The scripture reports that "this rumour of him went forth throughout all Judea, and throughout all the region round about." They knew what he had done and told all who would listen.

The accounts give no further knowledge of the mother in the story, or of her son. Perhaps they believed on Christ and followed him, but even this is not recorded. The raising of the widow's son was a visual sign to Israel that Jesus was the Messiah, and by this sign to his covenant people—a people who should have readily recognized it—Jesus declared, "I am he."

The Feeding of the Five Thousand

John 6:1—15

1. After these things Jesus went over the sea of Galilee, which is the sea of Tiberias.

2. And a great multitude followed him, because they saw his miracles which he did on them that were diseased.

3. And Jesus went up into a mountain, and there he sat with his disciples.

4. And the passover, a feast of the Jews, was nigh.

5. When Jesus then lifted up his eyes, and saw a great company come unto him, he saith unto Philip, Whence shall we buy bread, that these may eat?

6. And this he said to prove him: for he himself knew what he would do.

7. Philip answered him, Two hundred pennyworth of bread is not sufficient for them, that every one of them may take a little.

8. One of his disciples, Andrew, Simon Peter's brother, saith unto him,

9. There is a lad here, which hath five barley loaves, and two small fishes: but what are they among so many?

10. And Jesus said, Make the men sit down. Now there was much grass in the place. So the men sat down, in number about five thousand.

11. And Jesus took the loaves; and when he had given thanks, he distributed to the disciples, and the disciples to them that were set down; and likewise of the fishes as much as they would.

12. When they were filled, he said unto his disciples, Gather up the fragments that remain, that nothing be lost.

13. Therefore they

gathered them together, and filled twelve baskets with the fragments of the five barley loaves, which remained over and above unto them that had eaten.

14. Then those men, when they had seen the miracle that Jesus did, said,

This is of a truth that prophet that should come into the world.

15. When Jesus therefore perceived that they would come and take him by force, to make him a king, he departed again into a mountain himself alone.

Cross-references:

Matthew 14:13—22   Mark 6:32—45
Luke 9:10—17   JST Mark 6:36   JST Luke 9:13

This is the only specific miracle reported by all four Gospel writers. John is here used as the principal scriptural reference. There are only slight variances in the texts, and these variances are of no significance to the miracle's outcome or purpose. There are, however, varied circumstances reported about the events in the Lord's ministry immediately preceding the miracle. These differences can, in all probability, be attributed to the independent authorship of the Gospels. The scripture indicates that Jesus wanted solitude and seclusion from the crowds, desiring to get away privately with the Twelve. They left to find seclusion in the dry, uncultivated mountains of the Holy Land.

But privacy was not to be Christ's on this occasion, for the Gospels all agree that a multitude followed him. John reports that at this time the feast of the Passover was nigh, which would have brought large crowds of people to and from Jerusalem. The annual event was the most important of the Jewish religious celebrations, and according to Josephus, "an innumerable multitude of people" thronged Jerusalem for this feast.[8] Josephus reports that Cestius once took a census of Jerusalem at the time of the Passover to inform Nero of the city's power. Cestius asked the high priests to number the multitude, which they did by counting the sacrifices slain at the feast (256,500). They then estimated that ten or eleven people would celebrate each sacrifice. (It was not lawful for anyone to feast singly, and some companies were known to include as many as twenty.) From this the priests reported that 2,700,200 Jews had come to the feast "pure and holy." (Those who were "unclean" could not sacrifice, nor could any foreigners, so the figure computed was below the actual total.)[9] Thus, for Christ to have five thousand men (plus women and children) follow him at this time in no way stretches the imagination.

The reason why such a large multitude followed Jesus into the wilderness area is scripturally recorded. There is no doubt that by this time in the Lord's ministry he had attracted much attention. He had performed many miracles. He had healed the sick and raised the dead, and his fame had been spread abroad. John notes that the great multitude followed Christ "because they saw his miracles which he did on them that were diseased." Matthew reports that upon seeing the multitude that had followed him, Jesus "was moved with compassion toward them, and he healed their sick." Luke confirms this, reporting that Jesus "spake unto them of the kingdom of God, and healed them that had need of healing." Wherever Christ went, the people, hearing of his presence, brought to him their sick and diseased to have them healed. It was so here, and the Master did not disappoint them.

This was a Jewish multitude, and the miracle required that it be so. The Passover feast and the proximity to Jerusalem would itself attest to the crowd's "Jewishness." But there are also verifying circumstances within the miracle itself. One evidence surfaces when the blessing of the food in this miracle is compared with the prayer in the feeding of the four thousand (see Matthew 15:32—38; Mark 8:1—9). There was but one blessing here, "in strict accordance with Jewish custom," whereas the bread and fish were blessed separately for the four thousand. Only one prayer was to be uttered for a Jewish meal; to do otherwise would have given offense to the Jews, and they would not have eaten.[10] But it is the multitude's reaction that finally verifies their Jewish nationality and reveals the major purpose for recording the miracle.

Mark records that Jesus, upon seeing the multitude, had compassion not only for their physical illnesses but also for their spiritual maladies. He referred to them as "sheep not having a shepherd: and he began to teach them many things." They had all come with enthusiasm "taking no thought, for the time at least, of what they should eat or what they should drink, only desirous to hear the word of life, only seeking the kingdom of heaven;"[11] and no preparation had been made for their earthly needs.

The physical proceedings of the miracle are well defined by the Gospel writers. The disciples were concerned over the length of time the crowd had spent with Jesus. They requested the Lord to dismiss the people so that they might adequately provide for their own physical needs. But the Lord had other intentions. He asked of Philip, although it was intended for all the Twelve, "Whence shall we buy bread, that these may eat?" John reports that Christ did this to "prove him," for "he himself knew what he would do."

The question required the Twelve to anticipate certain conclusions about Jesus. They had seen evidence of his Messiahship, but dare they conclude that he would feed the multitude in the wilderness as Jehovah had done of old? The "proving" of the multitude would come after the miracle. Would they recognize in the miracle the witness of his divinity and acknowledge his Messiahship? It was the Passover, the event that more than any other brought to remembrance Jehovah's promise to Israel that the Messiah would come. This event celebrated Israel's deliverance from bondage; now, as then, Israel desired and needed that hoped-for deliverance and looked for him who would provide it. Jesus again provided a witness of his divinity by stirring Israel's memory of Old Testament anticipations.

Exodus 16:1—35. After Moses had delivered the children of Israel from slavery in Egypt, his problems were not ended. Although the people were free, they were distraught because they were hungry. They murmured against Moses and Aaron and wished that they had died in Egypt, for there they "did eat bread to the full." But now Moses and Aaron had taken them into the wilderness, "to kill this whole assembly with hunger." Moses inquired of the Lord and was told," I will rain bread from heaven for you." The people were instructed to gather all they needed each day, but no more. The next morning, after the dew had passed, "there lay a small round thing" on the ground, and the people said to one another, "It is manna." It tasted like wafers made with honey and it appeared white, like coriander seed.

Israel was to keep an "omer" full of the manna from generation to generation that their children could "see the bread wherewith I [the Lord] have fed you."

But in the wilderness the people tired of manna and demanded meat. The Lord, disgusted by their ungratefulness, provided quail for them by a wind from the sea, for "even a whole month, until it come out at your nostrils" (see Numbers 11:4–20). Thereafter "the children of Israel did eat manna forty years."

1 Kings 17:8–16. The prophet Elijah also provided food miraculously. When Elijah arrived at the home of the widow whom Jehovah had prepared to sustain him, he asked for a drink and for bread to eat. The widow responded that she had but a small portion of meal and oil left, and was about to prepare it for herself and her son so that they might eat it and die. Elijah told her to prepare it for him instead and to fear not, for "the barrel of meal shall not waste, neither shall the cruse of oil fail, until the day that the Lord sendeth rain upon the earth," and it was so.

2 Kings 4:39–44. Elisha miraculously provided for the people by first neutralizing a pot of inadvertently poisoned food so that all could eat. Then a servant brought to Elisha "twenty loaves of barley, and full ears of corn in the husks thereof." Elisha commanded the servant to feed the people. The servant immediately questioned the command of Elisha, for there were "an hundred men." Elisha again ordered the feeding, and the servant complied. The men ate, were filled, and had food left over.

From this heritage Jesus roused the multitude's memory and again declared his Messiahship to the people.

Philip's response to the Lord's question of how they could feed the multitude addressed the impossibility of purchasing so much food as to provide for the people. "Two hundred pennyworth of bread is not sufficient for them, that every one of them may take a little," he responded. After noting a meager provision of only five barley loaves and two small fishes, Andrew asked, "But what are they among so many?" Jesus instructed the disciples to seat the multitude in companies of hundreds and fifties on the grass, presumably for order and convenience, and this was done. The Lord then blessed—in the Jewish manner—the food to be partaken of, and gave it to the disciples to distribute to the people. As with the manna, the meal and the oil, and the bread and corn of Old Testament remembrance, the food multiplied and all were fed. And, as in the case of Elisha and the bread and corn, all were filled. Indeed, enough extra was gathered to fill twelve baskets.

How did the Lord perform this miracle? Obviously he used his creative power, but the actual process eludes the mortal mind. The important fact is that the miracle did occur. The people could not help but associate this miracle with those miraculous feedings of old. Jesus was recalling to the people's memory the great expectations they held for their awaited Messiah. The multitude recognized and remembered.

John records that those men who had witnessed the miracle said, "This is of a truth that prophet that should come into the world." What the disciples may not have dared recognize before the miracle, the people openly acknowledged afterward.

What then occurred is most significant. The multitude recognized in Jesus their looked-for Messiah. But what Messiah did they expect? The national conception of the Messiah involved political and material power. Moral reform and spiritual power were not expected to be the primary goals of the Messianic triumph (see chapter 1). Jesus perceived that the people were going to take him by force "to make him a king." It was not the character of Jesus that aroused the multitude to this reaction, but the influence of his miracle. The effect on the crowd was in keeping with the ideas of the time, but Jesus would not comply with their wishes. His was not an earthly kingdom, but a heavenly one. He was not sent to fill their material needs, but to fulfill their spiritual needs. His purpose was to save not the body but the soul. After constraining his disciples to leave and dismissing the multitude, Jesus "departed again into a mountain himself alone."

Accounts of the miraculous feeding of the five thousand no doubt spread abroad to increase Christ's fame, as did the interpretation of the miracle as well. John reports (see John 6) that later the people sought Jesus and found him, but Jesus recognized their intent and stated that they had come because of the bread and the miracles and not because of his teachings. They then asked for a sign—the Messianic sign. The miraculous providing of bread and fish was accepted, but it was not unique. They reminded him that their fathers had been given bread from heaven. Jesus quickly emphasized that it was not Moses who gave the bread, but his Father. Then followed the sermon on the bread of life.

The people had correctly interpreted the miracle and looked to Christ to confirm his Messiahship, but they still sought the coming of the politically all-powerful Messiah. A second sign had been given, and by it once more he had declared, "I am he."

Summary

The Jews had received two great signs. Other miracles had been or would be publicly performed, but not with the same emphasis. In the raising of the widow's son and the feeding of the five thousand, the Gospel writers recorded Christ's open, public claim to his people that he was their expected Messiah.

The chosen people had been taught for centuries to expect the Messiah. The signs of his coming had been impressed upon the people and taught in every home. Jesus came to them, doing what they expected of him, yet they missed him; not because they did not make the association or recognize his claim, but because they had overshot the mark. They were so concerned about their material condition, their needed relief from Rome and other enemies, and their day-to-day activities, that they had transposed the signs of his two comings. They sought the second coming of the Messiah in all his power and glory, not his first coming, in which he would establish his spiritual kingdom, the kingdom that would, if accepted and followed, allow entry into his final kingdom.

The people gladly accepted his miracles, they rejoiced in the healing of their sick and diseased, they glorified God when he restored them to life, and they satisfied their hunger with his bread and fish; but they would not accept his spiritual offerings. They asked for a sign. He gave them two, and they rejected them both.

Recognized by Demons, Accused by His Own

Before discussing the following three miracles, all of which deal with possession, it would be beneficial to discuss evil spirits in general. This is a difficult subject, and without a knowledge of man's true relationship to the spirit world it would be impossible to arrive at any realistic understanding of the problems, circumstances, and purposes of possession, and the miracles of removing evil spirits from the possessed.

The source of evil, wicked, and unclean spirits. In the beginning, before the creation of the physical earth, mankind existed as spirit children of our Heavenly Father. It was this Father who spoke to Adam and Eve in the Garden of Eden and who attested to the divinity of his Only Begotten Son both at the baptism of Jesus and on the Mount of Transfiguration. There, in the premortal existence, we were all spirits, with the exception of our heavenly parents. The spirit beings did not have physical bodies, although they appeared much as man does now, but in spiritual tabernacles.

Many "noble and great ones" (see Abraham 3:22–23) were present who would later in their physical bodies occupy positions of authority and power on the earth. Jesus was present and was known by the name Jehovah. Michael and Gabriel were there also, and some of their activities are recorded in the scriptures. All who would come to this earth were with them. So was another important figure. Isaiah called him Lucifer, a son of the morning (see Isaiah 14:12). John the Revelator referred to him as "a great red dragon" (see Revelation 12:3). He too was a spirit son of our Heavenly Father. All the spirits progressed in this pre-earthly existence under the tutelage of our Heavenly Father. At a certain point in that progression, a great council was called. All spirits who could potentially belong to this earth were present. There the Father's plan for mortality was presented.

At this council, Lucifer objected to the Father's plan. He presented an alternate one, one that opposed the Father's; and he said in his heart, "I will ascend into heaven, I will exalt my throne above the stars of God: . . . I will ascend above the heights of the clouds; I will be like the most High" (Isaiah 14:13—14). His plan was rejected by God, but he nevertheless convinced a large host to follow him. John tells us that this host consisted of "the third part of the stars [spirit children of God] of heaven" (Revelation 12:4). Because of his disobedience to the plan of the Father, he failed in his "first estate" (the premortal, spiritual existence, see Abraham 3:26), and he was punished, along with those that followed him, by being "cast . . . to the earth" (see Revelation 12:9), never to receive a tabernacle of flesh and never to have any further opportunity to reenter the Father's kingdom. When he rebelled against God, he was cast down, and "he became Satan, yea, even the devil, the father of all lies" (Moses 4:4). Thereafter, he and his angels had but one purpose—"to deceive and to blind men, and to lead them captive at his will, even as many as would not hearken unto my [God's] voice" (Moses 4:4).

Some of the devil's exploits with man upon the earth are described in the scriptures. In the Garden of Eden he tempted Adam and Eve and persuaded them to disobey God's commandment, and thus they became separated from God (see Moses 4; Genesis 3). He came to Moses and tempted him (see Moses 1:12—22), and he personally appeared to Jesus in an attempt to bring down the Savior of the World (see Matthew 4:1—11; Mark 1:12—13; Luke 4:1—13). Men sin, which is evil. If a man knows God's laws, the evil that he commits is his own responsiblity; nevertheless, all evil emanates from one source, i.e., the devil and his angels, that third part of heaven's host that was cast down to the earth. Indeed, Jewish theologians believed in only two sources of power in the supernatural world: God, from whom emanated all good; and Satan, from whom came all evil.

What did possession mean? The Jews taught and believed that a wicked or unclean spirit could physically possess a human body.[1] Once that possession had taken place, the "demon"—as such a spirit was sometimes called—could then take control of the speech, arms, legs, and other functions of the body, thus causing a person to do and say things that normally he or she would not. Such a person did not become a servant of Satan, subjectively and willingly doing his will; rather he was possessed by an evil spirit, and therefore lost control of his will and could not act independently from the demon.

This describes possession generally, but it is obvious from the New Testament accounts that different degrees of possession occurred, and that at times the possessed person could reassert himself, and his conscious self would prevail, at least momentarily.

The recorded occurrences indicate that a possessed person was obviously in bondage, did not have control of his normal functions, did not control his bodily activities and behavior, often hurt or injured himself, was considered "unclean," caused fear in others, and had his life cruelly shattered. He endured the real presence of another will from an alien power whose influence and will was set against all righteousness. Not all scriptural instances of possession record physical abuse of the host, but enough do that the question is raised of why a demon spirit, so desirous of possessing the body of another, should be so bent on destroying that same body.

No conclusive scriptural answer is given for this phenomenon. Logic could indicate that the evil spirit is so determined to enforce its will on its host that it would do so even by physical means. But the possessed person is not in a hopeless condition. His is "not . . . the deliberate giving in to Satanic will, of an utterly lost soul, but, in many instances at least, the still recoverable wreck of what might once have been a noble spirit."[2]

The causes of possession. The causes of possession in scripture arouse much thought. Undoubtedly sin—disobedience to God's law—plays a part in allowing a person to become possessed. But occasionally evil spirits have physically attacked righteous men as well.[3] Certainly the sins of those possessed, as recorded in scripture, were not beyond the Lord's mercy. Yet it can also be assumed that by gradual degrees one can choose wickedness so as to become virtually a captive of its author, the devil. Although not possessed, such was apparently the case with Korihor, who was stricken dumb for his arrogant rebellion and recalcitrance. His plea for restoration of speech was denied because, as the prophet Alma told him, if the curse were to be taken away he would return to his former wickedness (see Alma 30). Presumably those the Savior relieved of demoniac possession were not in this category, yet they may have tampered with sin in such kind and degree as to permit the entrance of an evil spirit, though not entirely lost to desires for righteousness.

In Jewish thought many diseases were connected with possession.[4] However, it would be unrealistic, then as well as now, to infer that those diseases referred to in the New Testament in association with possession were caused by evil. An example of this is the infirmity described as being "dumb," which included speech impediments as well as the inability to speak at all. At times this was connected with possession, as in Matthew chapters 9 and 12, although the same infirmity, recorded by Mark in chapter 7, is not associated with possession.

The experiences cited in the New Testament and our knowledge of Satan's purpose verify that possession is real. That sin affects possession and righteousness prevents it would be an obvious conclusion. But we cannot conclude that possession automatically means total wickedness and subservience to Satan any more than we can automatically conclude that any individual sin caused the possession.

It is evident that sin could be involved with possession, yet the sin would not have to be unforgivable or a sin that divine intervention could not overcome. The possessed soul could yet be allowed to come back into conformity with God's laws and be permitted entrance into the Lord's kingdom.

What about possessions today? Considering the many experiences recorded or alluded to in the New Testament, why are there no such possessions today; or if there are, why are they not as numerous or as readily recognized?

Most Christian writers seem to agree that the problem of possession was more prevalent at the time of Christ.[5] Consider the following reasons. First, it was the time of the coming of the Son of Man in the flesh. The advocate of evil over good would logically exert a strong influence at the time when the presence of Christ was near. Also, the spiritual state of the chosen people was at a very low ebb. Apparently it had been over four hundred years since the last prophet of the Old Testament, and apostasy was rampant.

Second, this was the time when the mission of Christ would overcome the results of sin, i.e., death. Until the advent of Christ, death conquered all men, and in death the devil found momentary success over the power of God. In Christ all would be made alive, and in him death had no power. Therefore, thwarting Jesus' purpose and mission was a prime objective of the devil.

Third was the belief of the Jews themselves. As already noted, they believed in only two sources of supernatural power—God and Satan.[6] Once Christ made his claim to the Messiahship, they must accept his powers as being from one or the other of these sources. Once they rejected him, the only argument left was that the power he exercised was of the devil. With the great powers of evil so prevalent, the potential for confusing the people was even greater.

Summary. The New Testament writings must stand for what they are and what they represent. No attempt should be made to place modern rationale upon the narrations concerning demoniacs. The scriptural examples of demoniac possession enhance our awareness of evil spirits. That awareness should lead to an increased understanding of the world of evil beyond the physical world and its potential influence upon man. The door through which these worlds connect is within each individual. It is our own negligence or willfulness that allows that door to open for evil to enter and possess that which God has given.

The Demoniac in the Synagogue at Capernaum

Mark 1:21—28

21. And they went into Capernaum; and straightway on the sabbath day he entered into the synagogue, and taught.

22. And they were astonished at his doctrine: for he taught them as one that had authority, and not as the scribes.

23. And there was in their synagogue a man with an unclean spirit; and he cried out,

24. Saying, Let us alone; what have we to do with thee, thou Jesus of Nazareth? art thou come to destroy us? I know thee who thou art, the Holy One of God.

25. And Jesus rebuked him, saying, Hold thy peace, and come out of him.

26. And when the unclean spirit had torn him, and cried with a loud voice, he came out of him.

27. And they were all amazed, insomuch that they questioned among themselves, saying, What thing is this? what new doctrine is this? for with authority commandeth he even the unclean spirits, and they do obey him.

28. And immediately his fame spread abroad throughout all the region round about Galilee.

Cross-reference

Luke 4:31—37

This miracle is the first specific New Testament recording of the confrontation between Christ and one who was possessed. Both Mark and Luke record the occurrence; Mark is used here as the primary account. He records that Jesus was teaching in the synagogue at Capernaum on the Sabbath day and the people were "astonished at his doctrine." They were astonished because he spoke with "authority, and not as the scribes." The scribes spoke of probabilities and opinions. Here the people's response indicated that they recognized Christ's Messianic claims, for the Pharisees and scribes taught that only God could speak with authority.[7]

The scripture reports that there was one "with an unclean spirit" in the synagogue. Apparently his presence was known but not forbidden. The unclean spirit cried out while Jesus was teaching. Note that it was not the person in whom the spirit resided, but the evil spirit itself, speaking through the voice of the possessed person. He recognized Jesus and cried out, "Let us alone." There is no scriptural evidence that this was a multiple possession; therefore, the evil spirit was apparently referring to the general condition of the host of spirits that had been cast down to the earth from the presence of the Father.

The spirit continued, "What have we to do with thee, thou Jesus of Nazareth? art thou come to destroy us?" His expectations were self-contained and self-fulfilling. He knew that Jesus could and would eventually destroy his kingdom. The spirit continued, "I know thee who thou art, the Holy One of God."

This spirit had been in that great council in heaven before the world was. He had been present when the Father had presented his plan and asked, "Whom shall I send?" Jesus had answered, "Here am I, send me." When the second responded—with like words but evil intentions—the Father rejected him, and he, Lucifer, became angry "and kept not his first estate; and, at that day, many followed after him" (Abraham 3:27—28; see Isaiah 6:8; 14:12—16). He who was now addressing the Savior was one of those who had become rebellious, as Satan did, and followed the devil, to torment man and to oppose the very Son of God. The demoniac knew Jesus from that great council, knew that He had been chosen of God, and knew that His authority far exceeded that of his master, the devil; so he asked, "Art thou come to destroy us?" Jesus now rebuked the evil spirit, saying "Hold thy peace, and come out of him."

The evil spirit could not disobey. He once again agonized the possessed, and after he "had torn him, and cried with a loud voice, he came out of him." Luke indicates that he did not physically hurt his victim, but tormented the possessed for one last time before leaving; then he obeyed and left.

The people who witnessed the cleansing were amazed at what had happened. The Jews believed in possession and had procedures for cleansing, described at times by the word *exorcism*.[8] But with the Christ it was different. He had merely to command and the unclean spirit would depart. The people recognized this, for they said, "What new doctrine is this? for with authority commandeth he even the unclean spirits, and they do obey him." And they spread his fame abroad.

Another witness to the people of Christ's Messiahship had taken place. Jesus, by his command, evidenced his authority over evil. The people had difficulty in recognizing Jesus for who he was; only those who believed could do so. But the evil spirits had no such limitation. They knew him from before and, unlike mortals, had not had a veil drawn over their memories of pre-earth events. They knew exactly who Jesus was, and in accordance with the order of things, they acknowledged it. But the people must recognize him from the good, not from the evil. So Jesus rebuked the evil spirit and would not allow him to speak.

This was the first public confrontation between the two worlds of Jewish thought—good and evil, the two great influences that affected all of Jewish life. Jesus had been publicly recognized by the lesser of these two worlds as the supreme being that he was. The people knew that the demoniac was possessed. Jesus publicly commanded the evil spirit to leave; it acknowledged his authority and departed. The sought-for Messiah was directly assaulting the world of evil; it was now for the people to choose which they would follow.

One Possessed and Dumb

Matthew 9:32—33

32. As they went out, behold, they brought to him a dumb man possessed with a devil.

33. And when the devil was cast out, the dumb spake: and the multitudes marvelled, saying, It was never so seen in Israel.

Matthew 12:22—23

22. Then was brought unto him one possessed with a devil, blind, and dumb: and he healed him, insomuch that the blind and dumb both spake and saw.

23. And all the people were amazed, and said, Is not this the son of David?

Luke 11:14

14. And he was casting out a devil, and it was dumb. And it came to pass, when the devil was gone out, the dumb spake; and the people wondered.

The Beelzebub Argument

Matthew 12:24—45

24. But when the Pharisees heard it, they said, This fellow doth not cast out devils, but by Beelzebub the prince of the devils.

25. And Jesus knew their thoughts, and said unto them, Every kingdom divided against itself is brought to desolation; and every city or house divided against itself shall not stand:

26. And if Satan cast out Satan, he is divided against himself; how shall then his kingdom stand?

27. And if I by Beelzebub cast out devils, by whom do your children cast them out? therefore they shall be your judges.

28. But if I cast out devils by the Spirit of God, then the kingdom of God is come unto you.

29. Or else how can one enter into a strong man's house, and spoil his goods, except he first bind the strong man? and then he will spoil his house.

30. He that is not with me is against me; and he that gathereth not with me scattereth abroad.

31. Wherefore I say unto you, All manner of sin and blasphemy shall be forgiven unto men: but the blasphemy against the Holy Ghost shall not be forgiven unto men.

32. And whosoever speaketh a word against the Son of man, it shall be forgiven him: but whosoever speaketh against the Holy Ghost, it shall not be forgiven him, neither in this world, neither in the world to come.

33. Either make the tree good, and his fruit good; or else make the tree corrupt, and his fruit corrupt: for the tree is known by his fruit.

34. O generation of vipers, how can ye, being evil, speak good things? for out of the abundance of the heart the mouth speaketh.

35. A good man out of the good treasure of the heart bringeth forth good things: and an evil man out of the evil treasure bringeth forth evil things.

36. But I say unto you, That every idle word that men shall speak, they shall give account thereof in the day of judgment.

37. For by thy words thou shalt be justified, and by thy words thou shalt be condemned.

38. Then certain of the scribes and of the Pharisees answered, saying, Master, we would see a sign from thee.

39. But he answered and said unto them, An evil and adulterous generation seeketh after a sign; and there shall no sign be given to it, but the sign of the prophet Jonas:

40. For as Jonas was three days and three nights in the whale's belly; so shall the Son of man be three days and three nights in the heart of the earth.

41. The men of Nineveh shall rise in judgment with this generation, and shall condemn it: because they repented at the preaching of Jonas; and, behold, a greater than Jonas is here.

42. The queen of the south shall rise up in the judgment with this gener-ation, and shall condemn it: for she came from the uttermost parts of the earth to hear the wisdom of Solomon; and, behold, a greater than Solomon is here.

43. When the unclean spirit is gone out of a man, he walketh through dry places, seeking rest, and findeth none.

44. Then he saith, I will return into my house from whence I came out; and when he is come, he findeth it empty, swept, and gar-nished.

45. Then goeth he, and taketh with himself seven other spirits more wicked than himself, and they enter in and dwell there: and the last state of that man is worse than the first. Even so shall it be also unto this wicked generation.

Cross-references

Matthew 9:34   Mark 3:22—30   Luke 11:15—26
John 10:19—21   JST Matthew 12:19—23, 26, 37—39
JST Mark 3:21—25   JST Luke 11:15, 20, 27

This miracle is unique and distinctive, but not because of the miracle itself, for the two Synoptics leave out all but the barest of detail concerning it. It is specifically mentioned and identified here not for its miraculous contents but for its consequences. This miracle precipitates one of the few direct arguments of record between Jesus and the Jewish rulers.

The miracle occupies only one verse in Luke, who merely states that Jesus was "casting out a devil, and it was dumb. . . . And the people wondered." Matthew writes only four verses about it; however, these four verses need some additional explanation. As noted, two verses appear in each of two different chapters, and it would seem that these verses describe the same event, even though they were recorded at different times. Both describe the cure of a dumb demoniac. (In chapter 12 he is also described as blind, which might be merely a condensation of the prelude of the miracle in chapter 9).[9]

The possessed person was brought to Jesus, who healed him. The multitude marveled, as in Luke, but Matthew further records the multitude as saying, "It was never so seen in Israel." Chapter 12 enlarges the multitude's comment, and the amazed people proclaim, "Is not this the son of David?" Thus, they attribute the Messianic position to Jesus. These glimpses, although brief, extol the miracle's virtues and authenticity.

The Beelzebub argument. The previous miracles performed by Jesus drew multitudes to him. The people "wondered, marveled, and were astonished." But his success angered his enemies, and in an attempt to discredit him they contrived an accusation against Jesus that became their defense to his miracles. The accusation centered on the source of his authority and power, and is referred to here as the Beelzebub argument. The scribes and Pharisees (the Jewish leadership) accused Jesus of casting out devils by the authority of the prince of devils, or Satan. The accusation was undoubtedly made on several occasions, but the Gospel writers selected the occasion of this miracle to record it. Undoubtedly, to some degree the Beelzebub argument blunted the people's acceptance of Christ, for it gave them an alternative to believe in and thus confused them.

The Jewish leadership did not want Jesus to be the Messiah, even though all of the signs and wonders pointed to that fact. By refusing to accept him as the Messiah they had only one alternative—to accuse him of performing such feats by the power of Beelzebub, the prince of devils; and accuse him they did!

The Beelzebub argument is found in all four Gospels, although two of the writers excluded the miracle of the one possessed and dumb. The Beelzebub argument struck at the very heart of Judaism. It was the classic confrontation between Jesus' establishing his claim as the Messiah and the Jewish leadership's rejecting it, and doing so in such a manner that would also persuade the people to reject him. Matthew 12:24—45 is the scriptural reference used here in discussing the Beelzebub argument.

The Jewish leadership had undoubtedly awaited such an opportunity as Jesus' miracle for the possessed and dumb man to put this cunning argument to the people. As the people marveled and exclaimed, "Is not this the son of David?" the scribes and Pharisees raised the challenge of his authority: "This fellow doth not cast out devils, but by Beelzebub the prince of devils."

Jesus, perceiving their thoughts, defended himself against their accusation. His answer was simple and direct: "Every kingdom [or house] divided against itself is brought to desolation; . . . and if Satan cast out Satan, . . . how shall then his kingdom stand?" His logic was unassailable. He acknowledged their belief and pronounced it correct: these powers came from only one of two sources—God or Satan. But he also reminded them that the two sources were mutually exclusive: God was always good, and Satan was always evil.

He emphasized this with two examples. First, he declared that a good tree brings forth only good fruit, while an evil tree always brings forth evil fruit. Second, he declared that what is treasured in the heart comes out of the mouth: good treasure produces good things; evil treasure produces evil things. He then applied these examples directly to both the Jews' history and their current situation. They were the chosen people. Their history was full of miracles such as he had performed, and they had even seen some enacted by their own children (speaking of the children of Abraham, and not their literal children). Jesus then reasoned that if he cast out devils by Beelzebub and they were the same "good things" that their own prophets had done, by what authority had the children of Israel cast them out?

He had forced them to judge themselves by their own standards. They were familiar with the concept of the Spirit of God. They claimed to be the keepers of the kingdom of God. They had taught that all good things previously done by the chosen people were done in the name of God. Therefore, they should judge his miracles and teachings by that same standard and spirit. They had seen his works and heard his claims. The people recognized in him the very things expected of and looked for in the Messiah. Now the direct challenge, the alternative to his authority, or the devil, had been raised as the source of his power. But he had turned the argument upon its promulgators. He could not have spoken more clearly had he said, "I am your Messiah."

Jesus continued that if they made the comparisons and thus found his actions to be the same as those of their children—in that he had cast out devils by the Spirit of God—"then the kingdom of God is come unto you." In this direct confrontation with the Jewish leadership, Jesus drew his miracles and teachings into one overpowering argument. Simply put, he challenged them to test his claim by the Spirit; if they did, they would conclude that he was the Messiah.

Christ further emphasized his position by commenting on the sin against the Holy Ghost. It was a grievous sin, not to be forgiven. His chosen people were now flirting with that very sin. "He that is not with me is against me," he stated. They were either with him, or against him and with the devil. Jesus had turned the Beelzebub argument upon his accusers.

The Jewish leadership understood. The scriptures make this quite plain. After Jesus concluded the argument, they offered no rebuttal. They could not have done so, because they believed what Jesus was teaching. Left without alternatives, they responded in the only manner they could without accepting him. "Master, we would see a sign from thee." By this request they acknowledged that they understood his position. Jesus had completely and successfully refuted the very argument they had conceived to discredit him. Even those who had challenged him questioned inwardly their rejection of him, so they asked the Lord to show them a sign.

But they had seen multiple signs. They had just witnessed a miracle in which Jesus had cast out a devil. They wanted the Messianic sign of the coming of the Son of Man. They were still looking for the wrong coming.

As a result of this blatant display of disbelief, Jesus called the whole generation wicked and adulterous for seeking after signs. In this unusually harsh condemnation the Lord obviously included the specific sexual sin of adultery, but also a much broader condemnation applied. They had sought a particular sign (the sign of the coming of the Son of Man) and this displayed their complete lack of faith in him as the Messiah. Their sins and disbelief had caused them to reject him; they had changed the doctrines of the Mosaic Law; confused and "adulterated" them. Jesus could not give them the sign they sought. It was reserved for a later period. But he would give them a sign, one they knew and should have been looking for—the sign of the prophet Jonas. This sign, the final sign of his first coming, would prove to all believers that he had completed and fulfilled the mission of his first coming. Christ's resurrection was foreshadowed in the sign of the prophet Jonas.

The balance of the material is self-explanatory. Jesus contrasted the current generation with those of Nineveh and the queen of the south (Sheba), declaring those generations to be better than this one. He warned them of their spiritual darkness because they would not see.

Jesus concluded his argument with an analogy, pointing out what their future would be like if they did not accept him. The analogy was couched in the story of a man with an unclean spirit (like the one he had just evicted from the possessed dumb man). When the unclean spirit was gone out of the man, that spirit wandered, seeking rest and finding none. Similarly, Israel had been chosen from among all nations and people. Their former evils (unclean spirits) had been cast away, and great blessings had been given them. The evil spirit (the former status of Israel and its current apostasy) then returned to its "house" (the formerly possessed man) and found it clean, swept, and empty. It promptly found seven additional spirits, more evil than itself, and all entered to dwell there, leaving the man in a worse state than before. By the same token the Jews had been chosen of God, their sins put aside, correct principles given to them; and now they were offered the kingdom of God. All had been done to prepare them for the coming Messiah. If they rejected him now, they would be worse off than before. Jesus then closed with this binding promise: "Even so shall it be also unto this wicked generation."

This little miracle, so often excluded or generalized, led to the most open claim to the Messiahship that Jesus had yet made in his ministry. Other claims would come and more miracles would be given, but none would be clearer or more concise. Israel was the chosen people, and the Messiah had come as promised.

The Demoniac That Was Legion

Mark 5:1—20

1. And they came over unto the other side of the sea, into the country of the Gadarenes.

2. And when he was come out of the ship, immediately there met him out of the tombs a man with an unclean spirit,

3. Who had his dwelling among the tombs; and no man could bind him, no, not with chains:

4. Because that he had been often bound with fetters and chains, and the chains had been plucked asunder by him, and the fetters broken in pieces: neither could any man tame him.

5. And always, night and day, he was in the mountains, and in the tombs, crying, and cutting himself with stones.

6. But when he saw Jesus afar off, he ran and worshipped him,

7. And cried with a loud voice, and said, What have I to do with thee, Jesus, thou Son of the most high God? I adjure thee by God, that thou torment me not.

8. For he said unto him, Come out of the man, thou unclean spirit.

9. And he asked him, What is thy name? And he answered, saying, My name is Legion: for we are many.

10. And he besought him much that he would not send them away out of the country.

11. Now there was there nigh unto the mountains a great herd of swine feeding.

12. And all the devils besought him, saying, Send us into the swine, that we may enter into them.

13. And forthwith Jesus gave them leave. And the unclean spirits went out, and entered into the swine: and the herd ran violently down a steep place into the sea, (they were about two thousand;) and were choked in the sea.

14. And they that fed the swine fled, and told it in the city, and in the country. And they went out to see what it was that was done.

15. And they come to Jesus, and see him that was possessed with the devil, and had the legion, sitting, and clothed, and in his right mind: and they were afraid.

16. And they that saw it told them how it befell to him that was possessed with the devil, and also concerning the swine.

17. And they began to pray him to depart out of their coasts.

18. And when he was come into the ship, he that had been possessed with the devil prayed him that he might be with him.

19. Howbeit Jesus suffered him not, but saith unto him, Go home to thy friends, and tell them how great things the Lord hath done for thee, and hath had compassion on thee.

20. And he departed, and began to publish in Decapolis how great things Jesus had done for him: and all men did marvel.

Cross-references:

Matthew 8:28—34   Luke 8:26—39
JST Mark 5:11   JST Luke 8:33

All the synoptic Gospels report this miracle, but John excludes it. Mark and Luke give similar reports; Matthew condenses his account and reports two demoniacs, while the others report only one.[10]

The exact location of this miracle is difficult to determine. Mark and Luke record that it took place in the "country of the Gadarenes," Luke adding, "which is over against Galilee." Matthew notes it was in "the country of the Gergesenes." Scholarly historical writers have differed on the location because of the differences in the scriptural text.[11] Jesus may have come to the east shore of the lake to gain solitude, peace, and rest, for his previous day had been very rigorous. This miracle—the last in this series of demoniac miracles—further confirms the supremacy of Jesus over the world of evil spirits.

Immediately upon Christ's arrival, and as "he was come out of the ship," he encountered the demoniac. The detailed description offered by the Synoptics seems to describe the absolute epitome of possession. They described the demoniac in such words as "exceeding fierce," "no man might pass by the way," "dwelling among the tombs," "no man could bind him, no, not with chains," "neither could any man tame him," "cutting himself with stones," "had devils a long time," and "ware no clothes." This was an experience like no other, and the Gospel writers emphasized it. This was also a very public miracle, and Jesus placed no restrictions on its being recounted.

The demoniac had been possessed for some time and lived in the tombs. These tombs—described as "being either natural caves or recesses artificially hewn out of the rock, often so large as to be supported with columns, and with cells upon their sides for the reception of the dead"[12] —the Jews associated with the dwelling place of possessed persons and those who were unclean.[13]

The man lived naked, as a wild man, and the people were genuinely afraid of him. All those in the area knew of the demoniac, and no one doubted that he was possessed. He could not be controlled and had broken chains and fetters into pieces. This is the man that met Jesus as he disembarked from the ship.

The possessed ran to Jesus, fell down, and worshipped him. The reaction was plain and simple. From the example of the unclean spirit in Capernaum, it is evident that the evil spirits immediately recognized Jesus and were drawn to him, even though they dreaded his presence. The possessed man had no foreknowledge of Jesus or his works. The physical circumstances of his possession precluded that. He lived alone in the tombs, and the power of the demons over him was inexorable and so complete that his actions, perhaps for years, had been completely controlled by those who possessed him. The Gospel writers report that there were many evil spirits involved in this possession, and their control dominated the man's miserable existence.

The scriptural accounts next record a unique and interesting experience. Jesus and the evil spirit converse. Unlike his silencing of the evil spirit at Capernaum, where the Lord refused to allow open testimony of his divine calling by inhabitants of Satan's evil kingdom, he now permits conversation. The evil spirit openly acknowledges him. "What have I to do with thee, Jesus, thou Son of the most high God?" he cries out. Jesus does not forbid the testimony. The accusation contained within the Beelzebub argument could never again be substantiated. The evil spirit had recognized Christ as the Son of God, even if the people themselves did not. The demon then begs the Lord, "I adjure thee by God, that thou torment me not." Another account reports it as saying, "Art thou come hither to torment us before the time?" Perhaps both remarks were made, and perhaps from different evil spirits. Again the comment goes unrebuked.

The Lord then continues the conversation. The demons will not be allowed to remain in the man. He commands them to come out of him and asks their name. This was not a stage healing. The evil spirits knew the Son of God and knew they could not stay in the body of him whom they had possessed for many years. The evil spirit responded and declared, "My name is Legion: for we are many."

The answer was clear. There were many evil spirits in this possession. Exactly how many is undetermined and unimportant. The message was that multiple evil spirits were in control of this one unfortunate man. Whether each was housed within the body at exactly the same time similarly does not matter.

Answering Christ's question with as much arrogance as he could, Luke reports that the evil spirit continued and "besought him that he would not command them to go out into the deep." Mark wrote that the plea was to "not send them away out of the country."

The Jews believed that certain countries were assigned to evil spirits and certain to good spirits. Once assigned to such a place a spirit could not pass beyond its boundaries.[14] The "deep," or "abyss," as it is sometimes translated, was that referred to by John in Revelation as the "bottomless pit" (see Revelation 9:1). From our knowledge of the final disposition of the devil and his angels and all those that follow him in this life, this "bottomless pit" would refer to "outer darkness," the final and last place reserved for those evil spirits.[15] To this place they knew that they must eventually be consigned, but they begged Jesus not to command them there "before the time."

Now for the final episode of the conversation. Apparently a herd of swine was grazing nearby. The evil spirits "besought him, saying, Send us into the swine." The wording differs slightly in the Gospel accounts, but the meaning is clear. They knew that their stay in the man was over, and rather than not possess *any* body, they preferred to inhabit the bodies of the swine. Jesus "gave them leave," and they pressed their influence upon the swine.

Did they physically enter the bodies of the swine? It is clear that the Gospel narrators wanted to leave that impression, for they say that the spirits "entered into the swine." However, whether the spirit bodies of the evil spirits entered and possessed the physical bodies of the swine is of no particular consequence, for the evil spirits' influence on the swine is amply attested to. In addition, the scripture testifies of the evil spirits' obsessive desire to exercise control over any body rather than none.[16]

The swine, which numbered two thousand, were not accustomed to such evil influence and ran violently to their deaths in the sea. The evil spirits were reduced to that spirit existence whence they came, to await the final judgment and their total banishment to outer darkness.

Those who witnessed this episode did not react unusually. The reports state that they were afraid, and no wonder! These were superstitious people. Jesus, whom they knew not, had been talking with a known demoniac, and then had cast the demons out of the man and allowed them to wreak their influence upon the swine, which promptly went berserk and plunged to their death in the sea. The witnesses ran to the nearby cities and told the story. Others came to see for themselves. What they saw was as astonishing to them as were the circumstances that brought it about. The demoniac was now calm, dressed, and sitting by Jesus, undoubtedly giving thanks to him who had released him from his torment.

Fear spread through them. Witnesses rehearsed to them all that had occurred, but to them it was incomprehensible. They could not understand this event and its significance. They could not comprehend the recovered soul now at Jesus' feet and the reasons for the dead swine. They were terribly frightened and were not knowledgeable of the Messiah and his work. Thus, they reacted quite normally under the circumstances. They asked Jesus to leave.

The Lord obliged them and prepared to depart. The demoniac, so recently relieved of his torture, requested permission to go with him to become a disciple; but Jesus said no. The purpose of the miracle demanded that he stay. The absolute relationship between Jesus and the evil spirits of that world controlled by Beelzebub, the prince of devils, had been illuminated. There was no question about who was subservient to whom. The evil spirits were totally subject to the will of Christ. The Beelzebub argument had been forever destroyed.

The restored demoniac was told to remain in his land and to tell the inhabitants about the great things the Lord had done for him. He was to be an instrument in the Lord's work. First, he would testify of the great miracle; the people could not refute it, for he was well known, and his testimony would glorify the Messiah. Second, he would become a missionary and would lay the groundwork among the inhabitants of his country for a greater reception of the Lord later on.

The man did as he was bid and departed, and "began to publish in Decapolis how great things Jesus had done for him." As a result "all men did marvel." In the future, Christ would return to this area (see Mark 6:53—56). The people would then no longer request that he leave, but would bring their sick from the entire region and would seek his healing power, and he would openly grant it to them.

Part Three

Jesus' Messiahship Witnessed to the Leaders

The Result of Verbal Claims

4

Passing Unseen (Before the Resurrection)

Luke 4:28–30

28. And all they in the synagogue, when they heard these things, were filled with wrath,

29. And rose up, and thrust him out of the city, and led him unto the brow of the hill whereon their city was built, that they might cast him down headlong.

30. But he passing through the midst of them went his way.

John 8:59

59. Then took they up stones to cast at him: but Jesus hid himself, and went out of the temple, going through the midst of them, and so passed by.

John 10:39

39. Therefore they sought again to take him: but he escaped out of their hand.

Sermon references associated with the miracle:

Luke 4:16—30   John 8:1—59   John 10:1—42

This is a unique miracle. It is not performed on anyone in particular, yet all in the vicinity are subject to it. "Passing unseen" describes incidents wherein Jesus was either not seen or not recognized even though he was in the midst of people who knew him. The examples of this miracle are divided into two categories: those that occurred before and those that occurred after the Resurrection (see chapter 12).

There are three separate occurrences of this miracle before the Resurrection. The setting for each of these situations is similar. Jesus delivers a sermon, and the sermon leads to the conclusion that he is the Son of God, the promised Messiah. In each instance the rulers of the Jews and others in the audience recognize his claim, become enraged, and seek to kill him. The miracle prevents them from accomplishing their intent.

The miracles of Jesus generally taught and testified of his divine calling; however, in these particular miracles it is not through the miracle itself that this is done. Here his sermons claim the Messiahship, and the miracle protects him from the crowd's angry reactions to those open claims.

A brief review of the sermons delivered prior to each unseen passing will help clarify the necessity and magnitude of the miracle. These sermons directly proclaim Jesus as the Messiah.

The first of these marvelous expositions takes place early in the Lord's ministry and is recorded by Luke. Jesus had returned to Nazareth, the place of his childhood. He was among the people who knew him as Jesus the carpenter, the son of Joseph and Mary. It was a Sabbath, and he was preparing to give a personal witness of his divinity to these hometown people. He would give this witness in the acceptable and traditional manner of the Jews: in the synagogue where the scribes, Pharisees, teachers, and rabbis gathered to teach and expound their religion to the people.[1]

Jesus stood up to read, the prescribed method for teaching in the synagogue. He was passed the book of the prophet Isaiah. He turned to what in our Bible is the sixty-first chapter and read verses one and two. It was a recognized Messianic passage. Upon completing the short reading he sat down, which was the signal that he was about to preach on the text he had read.

All eyes were fastened on him. He had performed many miracles before this time, and his fame had preceded him to Nazareth. However, his explanation of the passage was totally unexpected. He did not give a lengthy dissertation, but merely said, "This day is this scripture fulfilled in your ears." He had told them that he was the Messiah. They had heard of his wonders, his miracles, his mighty deeds, and now he openly declared that he was the Messiah they looked for. The people were stunned. Never had such a message been delivered in any synagogue in Israel. Luke's narrative describes their first response as wonder at "the gracious words."

Normally, the audience would have quickly discussed the teacher's comments among themselves and prepared to ask questions. But instead of inquiring about spiritual matters, they asked, "Is not this Joseph's son?" By this question they were rejecting the scriptural claim. They personally knew Jesus, and thus reasoned that he could not be the Messiah. Jesus responded, "No prophet is accepted in his own country" and continued with two pointed and significant analogies. He first recounted Elijah's rejection by the chosen people and reminded his audience that Sidon, a gentile city, accepted and cared for him. He then referred to Naaman, a Gentile, and pointed out that there were many lepers in Israel, but only Naaman was healed.

These examples filled the listeners with wrath. They knew his meaning in both instances. He had claimed to be the Messiah, and they had rejected him. He then compared their rejection of him to Elijah's rejection by ancient Israel, and reminded them that Naaman's faith in God's word was more than that of the chosen people. Thus Jesus accused them of being faithless and rejecting the chosen one of God. They rose up and "thrust him out of the city."[2] They did not care about their Sabbath law on this occasion, or any other law. They led him to a nearby hilltop with the malicious intent of killing him. They were going to "cast him down headlong" for what he had said. It was then that the miracle occurred. In the scripture it is almost neglected: "But he passing through the midst of them went his way." His time had not yet come. The bewilderment of the enraged crowd, though not recorded, must have been just as maddening as the circumstances that had brought them there, for he to whom this anger was directed was no longer among them.

John records both the remaining miracles in this category and the circumstances that led to them. The first is in John, chapter 8. Jesus had gone to the temple and had sat down to teach, as was the custom. The scheming scribes and Pharisees brought to him a woman who had been taken in adultery, apparently to ensnare him in some judgmental controversy of their law. He confounded them by requiring that "he that is without sin among you, let him first cast a stone at her." The accusers left. He dismissed the woman and admonished her to "sin no more."

But the Jewish leadership was relentless. They returned to speak more with him. Christ testified of his relationship with his Father, and they rejected that relationship, though not misunderstanding it. "We [are] Abraham's seed" and "Abraham is our father," they cried to him. Their response clearly indicated that they understood what Christ was saying. He had told them that God was his Father, and they had rejected it. He then perceived their thoughts and said, "But now ye seek to kill me." To their thinking he had blasphemed, and that meant death. Jesus renounced them, saying, "Ye are of your father the devil." Their intended sin of murder had condemned them.

Jesus again offered them spiritual clarity and eternal salvation. He told them that if they would yet believe, they should never see death. They responded by accusing Jesus of self-righteousness: "Art thou greater than our father Abraham, which is dead? and the prophets are dead: whom makest thou thyself?" Can there be any doubt that they understood?

Jesus continued expounding more on the relationship between him and his Father and declared, "Your father Abraham rejoiced to see my day: and he saw it, and was glad." By these words he clearly told them that in vision Abraham had seen, foretold, and rejoiced at the Savior's time.

Then in irreverent arrogance they responded, "Thou art not yet fifty years old, and hast thou seen Abraham?" Recognizing their contempt, Jesus openly declared, "Verily, verily, I say unto you, Before Abraham was, I am." This was clear: there could be no mistake. Moses, the great lawgiver, had asked the Lord what to tell the children of Israel that would prove to them that he represented their God. "What is his name?" he had asked. "I AM THAT I AM," Jehovah had responded. "Thus shalt thou say unto the children of Israel, I AM hath sent me unto you." (Exodus 3:13—14.) That same Jehovah was now upon the earth as the Messiah. This name and title of Jehovah (the Messiah) would have been readily recognized by the rulers of Israel. Thus, the King James rendering of Christ's statement could correctly read, "Verily, verily, I say unto you, Before Abraham, was I AM."[3]

Jesus had declared his Messiahship openly to this hostile crowd. Their reaction was deliberate. "Then took they up stones to cast at him." The evil he had discerned and perceived in their hearts now came out openly. They wanted to kill him. But again the miracle occurred: "Jesus hid himself, and went out of the temple, going through the midst of them, and so passed by." He did not hide from them and wait until they were gone. He passed unseen through their midst.

The final incident is recorded in John, chapter 10. Known generally as the Good Shepherd sermon, this is the most explicit of the confrontations between Christ and the Pharisees. The sermon is in two parts. The description of Christ as the shepherd and Israel as the sheep takes place in the first part of the sermon. Although important doctrinally and as background to the miracle, it is not this material that leads to the miracle. The miracle results from the second part of the sermon and the discussion that takes place between Jesus and the Pharisees.

Jesus was walking in the temple in the court called Solomon's porch when the Jews came to him and asked, "How long dost thou make us to doubt? If thou be the Christ, tell us plainly." Jesus was near the end of his ministry and would soon make his triumphant entry into Jerusalem. He had been ministering to them for almost three years. He had performed multitudes of miracles and testified to them many times. He had told them that he was the Christ. They had developed every means of diluting and rejecting his claim, yet because he was the Christ, the inner agony resulting from that rejection persisted in their minds and hearts. And so they requested of him candidly, "If thou be the Christ, tell us plainly."

The Lord's response was simple and just as pointed as the question. "I told you, and ye believed not." He continued, "The works that I do in my Father's name, they bear witness of me." Jesus repeated the analogy of the sheep and the shepherd, stating that his sheep hear his voice. He bore testimony that his Father had verified his works, and he concluded by stating, "I and my Father are one." He had again claimed the Messiahship. He had specifically been asked and had specifically answered.

The reaction was as before. "Then the Jews took up stones again to stone him." They would not have him as their Messiah. Jesus avoided the crowd's contention with a question: "Many good works have I shewed you from my Father; for which of those works do ye stone me?" They cited blasphemy as the reason: "because that thou, being a man, makest thyself God." They understood his claim, but refused to believe. In his final attempt to win them over, he concluded, "Say ye of him, whom the Father hath sanctified, and sent into the world, Thou blasphemest; because I said, I am the Son of God? If I do not the works of my Father, believe me not. But if I do, though ye believe not me, believe the works: that ye may know, and believe, that the Father is in me, and I in him."

It was too much. Their request for a plain answer had been fulfilled; indeed, the answer could not have been more plainly stated, yet they still would not accept it. "Therefore they sought again to take him: but he escaped out of their hand," and again passed unseen.

Jesus openly declared his Messiahship to the rulers of Israel: first, as the fulfillment of prophecy; second, by the recognition of his position and name; and third, by open declaration. Although the rulers recognized all three instances, they would have no part of him. They wanted to kill him, but his time was not yet; therefore, he passed unseen from their midst before their murderous desires could be fulfilled.[4]

Miraculous Conclusions

5

The Impotent Man at the Pool at Bethesda

John 5:1—16

1. After this there was a feast of the Jews; and Jesus went up to Jerusalem.

2. Now there is at Jerusalem by the sheep market a pool, which is called in the Hebrew tongue Bethesda, having five porches.

3. In these lay a great multitude of impotent folk, of blind, halt, withered, waiting for the moving of the water.

4. For an angel went down at a certain season into the pool, and troubled the water: whosoever then first after the troubling of the water stepped in was made whole of whatsoever disease he had.

5. And a certain man was there, which had an infirmity thirty and eight years.

6. When Jesus saw him lie, and knew that he had been now a long time in that case, he saith unto him, Wilt thou be made whole?

7. The impotent man answered him, Sir, I have no man, when the water is troubled, to put me into the pool: but while I am

coming, another steppeth down before me.

8. Jesus saith unto him, Rise, take up thy bed, and walk.

9. And immediately the man was made whole, and took up his bed, and walked: and on the same day was the sabbath.

10. The Jews therefore said unto him that was cured, It is the sabbath day: it is not lawful for thee to carry thy bed.

11. He answered them, He that made me whole, the same said unto me, Take up thy bed, and walk.

12. Then asked they him, What man is that which said unto thee, Take up thy bed, and walk?

13. And he that was healed wist not who it was: for Jesus had conveyed himself away, a multitude being in that place.

14. Afterward Jesus findeth him in the temple, and said unto him, Behold, thou art made whole: sin no more, lest a worse thing come unto thee.

15. The man departed, and told the Jews that it was Jesus, which had made him whole.

16. And therefore did the Jews persecute Jesus, and sought to slay him, because he had done these things on the sabbath day.

This is the first of three miracles discussed in this chapter. They were very public miracles, granted to people with well-known illnesses, and they confronted the religious leadership with the specific concept that Jesus was the Son of God.

John records that Jesus was at Jerusalem attending one of the feasts. John does not name the feast, nor is the current location of the pool known.[1]

John describes the pool as having a "great multitude of impotent folk, of blind, halt, [and] withered" around it. He was obviously describing a well-known area in Jerusalem. Not a "few" people surrounded the pool, but "a multitude." "Porches" had been constructed around three sides of the pool (undoubtedly constructed out of charity) to give some comfort to those who visited it, but the people were unattended. Israel's leaders, long ago charged with the care of such people, seemed to have ignored these poor folk. The pool and its inhabitants may well have been selected by the Lord to represent the spiritually impoverished condition of Israel. In the mysticism surrounding the water itself lies evidence of this condition. Those who waited did so for the water to be "troubled," apparently due to some physical condition of the water, probably a warm natural spring.[2] The water moved, or was "troubled," in an irregular pattern.

Verse 4 assists in the application of the preceding verses to Israel's spiritual condition. The superstition was that "an angel went down at a certain season into the pool, and troubled the water." Such superstitions were common in that day. The Jews believed in many kinds of angels, and all that was unexplained was attributed to the supernatural.[3] The people believed that once the pool was "troubled," "whosoever then first after the troubling of the water stepped in was made whole of whatsoever disease he had." This superstition would have developed naturally from the one that attributed the water's movement to angelic interference.

Israel's leaders had ignored the folk at the pool for a long time. The temple, the very symbol of Israel's favored position before God, was nearby. But the temple, with its formalism and indifference, was no longer representative of God's mercy to Israel. And there is no doubt that the elements of the temple glory no longer existed.

> The Holy of Holies was quite empty, the ark of the covenant, with the cherubim, the tables of the law, the book of the covenant, Aaron's rod that budded, and the pot of manna, were no longer in the sanctuary. The fire that had descended from heaven upon the altar was extinct. What was far more solemn, the visible presence of God in the Shechinah[4] was wanting. Nor could the will of God be ascertained through the Urim and Thummim, nor even the high-priest be anointed with the holy oil, its very composition being unknown. Yet all the more jealously did the Rabbis draw lines of fictitious sanctity, and guard them against all infringement.[5]

The attitude of the folk at the pool and the temple leaders who allowed such an attitude to exist was the true evidence that the superstition of the "troubled pool" held by the people and the religious fanaticism engendered by the temple could exist side by side.[6]

This miracle was not a frontal attack on the law—that would

come later. However it contrasted for the rulers and keepers of the law the purity and charity of the true kingdom of God with their own dead religion. Although the reason for Jesus' selecting this one man is not specifically recorded, it would appear that in him and his circumstance Jesus found the symbol that most accurately mirrored Israel's condition.

The impotent man "had an infirmity thirty and eight years." This length of time prevented any question of the authenticity of the miracle, but even this could have symbolized Israel's long-standing plight. Jesus spoke to the man at the pool with comfort and consolation. Yet his question—"Wilt thou be made whole?" —may seem almost superfluous.

Waiting as he had those many years, the impotent man was undoubtedly watching the water with intensity and may not have even noticed Jesus. His answer indicated his only concern, even though his healer stood before him. "I have no man," he stated, "to put me into the pool." The man, like Israel, was so intent upon a false hope that he did not (or could not) see salvation embodied in Christ's presence. The man may have thought that here was one that would help him into the pool at its next movement. His deep despair is echoed in his further response and plea: "While I am coming, another steppeth down before me." He displayed the anguish of one who had tried many times but was unable to reach his goal. The water would move and he would attempt, in his superstition, to enter the water first. But others, less afflicted, would rush in before him, leaving him to wait for yet another movement of the pool. He did not realize that true healing was not to be found in the water of the pool.

The Lord in his compassion commanded the impotent man, "Rise, take up thy bed, and walk." The man knew not who Jesus was and had no knowledge of his intentions. But he responded to the command without hesitation. The infirm immediately became firm, and he took up his bed and walked. Now Israel's rulers could respond to the question, "Wilt thou be made whole?"

Significantly, this miracle took place on the Sabbath. The Jews intercepted the man carrying his bed, and questioned him. They did not rejoice in his miraculous healing, for they were more concerned with the law. The man defended his actions by stating that he who had healed him had told him to carry the bed, thus removing himself from the vengeance of the Sabbath protectors. Their concern now turned from him who had been cured. Their religious fanaticism prevented them from understanding either his previous cry for help or his current expression of praise and joy. But the man did not know who had healed him, and Jesus had moved on, perhaps to avoid the confrontation between the man and the watchful Jews and to avoid the inevitable excitement of the miracle. Thus the man could not see or identify him.

Jesus did not allow his compassion for this man to go without proper spiritual attention. The man went to the temple, perhaps to give thanks, and Jesus found him there. The Lord told him he had been "made whole," to assure the man that his healing was complete. But he imparted a solemn warning: "Sin no more, lest a worse thing come unto thee." It appears that the man's affliction had been caused by his own actions, or perhaps his inability to get well had been hindered by his unfaithfulness. Whichever is the explanation, the man was admonished for contributing to his own sickness and was warned not to continue lest some worse result come.

At this point the man knew his benefactor. He immediately went to the Jewish leaders and told them. His reasons for doing so are not expressed. He may have felt some pressure because of the previous accusation against him by the rulers, but it would seem illogical to ascribe evil intent to his action. He had just been miraculously healed—physically and spiritually—after suffering thirty-eight years with both handicaps. In addition, he had been warned by one whose power he could not doubt that further evil would have even more serious consequences. Further, his very words seem to preclude such a conclusion. He told them "that it was Jesus, which had made him whole." Apparently he did not report that Jesus had told him to take up his bed, but only that he had healed him. Perhaps he hoped that they, too, might praise him.

But this was not to be. After finding out that Jesus had performed this miracle, they ignored the healed man altogether. They persecuted Christ and "sought to slay him, because he had done these things on the sabbath day." The miracle produced only anger and rejection in the Jewish leadership and further emphasized their spiritual darkness. As a response to their murderous intentions, Jesus told them, "My Father worketh hitherto, and I work" (John 5:17). The Jewish rulers recognized the comparison immediately, and "sought the more to kill him, because he not only had broken the sabbath, but said also that God was his Father, making himself equal with God" (John 5:18). With the rulers before him (brought there by the miracle), Jesus testified to his divine relationship with the Father and to his own works, including his Messiahship. His testimony was directed specifically to the rulers of Israel, pointed and self-fulfilling.

The response of the Jewish leaders only illustrated more vividly their failure to recognize the Master. The glory of the healer and his compassion was lost in the pompous observance of their perverted law. The impotent man at the pool had not recognized the Savior when he first spoke with him any more than Israel's leaders did now.

Through this miracle, Jesus once more offered to save the soul of Israel. He could have performed sign upon sign, day after day, until the leaders either tired of signs or ultimately believed. But the signs were merely the evidence of his presence among them. To recognize him required faith, and they lacked that faith. This impotent man's affliction mirrored Israel's. He exemplified the contrast between the kingdom of the Jews and the kingdom of God. Healing the impotent man was a significant example of Christ's compassion, but his was not a happenstance healing. It was a sign to be recognized and acknowledged.

The One Sick of the Palsy

Mark 2:1–12

1. And again he entered into Capernaum, after some days; and it was noised that he was in the house.

2. And straightway many were gathered together, insomuch that there was no room to receive them, no, not so much as about the door: and he preached the word unto them.

3. And they come unto him, bringing one sick of the palsy, which was borne of four.

4. And when they could not come nigh unto him for the press, they uncovered the roof where he was: and when they had broken it up, they let down the bed wherein the sick of the palsy lay.

5. When Jesus saw their faith, he said unto the sick of the palsy, Son, thy sins be forgiven thee.

6. But there were certain of the scribes sitting there, and reasoning in their hearts.

7. Why doth this man thus speak blasphemies? who can forgive sins but God only?

8. And immediately when Jesus perceived in his spirit that they so reasoned within themselves, he said unto them, Why reason ye these things in your hearts?

9. Whether is it easier to say to the sick of the palsy, Thy sins be forgiven thee; or to say, Arise, and take up thy bed, and walk?

10. But that ye may know that the Son of man hath power on earth to forgive sins, (he saith to the sick of the palsy,)

11. I say unto thee, Arise, and take up thy bed, and go thy way into thine house.

12. And immediately he arose, took up the bed, and went forth before them all; insomuch that they were all amazed, and glorified God, saying, We never saw it on this fashion.

Cross-references:

Matthew 9:1—8   Luke 5:17—26   JST Matthew 9:2, 5
JST Mark 2:3, 7   JST Luke 5:23—24

This miracle was performed in Capernaum, a city that Christ later said would be "brought down to hell" because it had rejected the many mighty miracles that had been performed there (see Matthew 11:23—24).

The circumstances of this miracle are quite different from those surrounding the healing of the impotent man by the pool. A comparison of the two is enlightening.

Impotent Man by the Pool

- Jesus seeks the man out
- Long illness

The One Sick of the Palsy

- The man seeks Jesus out
- Long illness

- No foreknowledge of Jesus
- Believes in the superstition that the pool can heal him
- Man questioned by rulers

- Physical healing first
- Spiritual healing private
- Physical healing public
- Jesus claims verbally to be the Son of God

- Miracle leads into teaching

- Knows of and believes in Jesus
- Believes Jesus can heal him

- Jesus perceives thoughts of questioning rulers
- Spiritual healing first
- Spiritual healing public
- Physical healing public
- Jesus forgives sins and thus claims to be equal with God
- Miracle confirms teaching

The miracle is recorded in all three synoptic Gospels; Mark will serve as the primary text.

Jesus had come to Capernaum several days before this miracle occurred, and it was "noised" about that he was there. The miracles Jesus had previously performed at Capernaum and elsewhere had by now made him famous. On this particular day, "straightway many were gathered together." Jesus was teaching, and many of the Jewish rulers were present. Mark and Matthew refer to them as scribes, while Luke identifies them as Pharisees and doctors of the law. Many of the common people were also present, such that "there was no room to receive them, no, not so much as about the door." The house could not hold all who wanted to hear, and they spilled out into the yard so that none could gain entry. No specifics on what Jesus was teaching are given. The scripture merely states that he preached the word unto them. Undoubtedly, he would have been teaching about the kingdom of God and its requirements.[7] But regardless of his subject matter, his preaching did not conclude in an ordinary manner.

Four good-hearted people were coming to Jesus carrying on a litter or bed one that was "sick of the palsy." They had heard that Jesus was there and wanted to get this man (whose soul was sick as well as his body) to Jesus. Upon arriving at the house they could see that entrance through the door was impossible; but undaunted, they chose an alternative method of reaching Jesus. The house (typical of the construction at the time) would have had a staircase in the rear leading to the roof. They proceeded to climb the stairs.[8] The four bearing the palsied man knew in which area Jesus was teaching. They immediately took their burden to the roof and commenced tearing a hole in the ceiling area. The intensity of their determination is revealed as the story unfolds. One can imagine that as the four began to open a hole in the roof, Jesus probably stopped speaking. All eyes would have focused on the noise overhead. Jesus would not have been offended at the disturbance. To the contrary, such determination could only be commended and rewarded. After uncovering the roof, the four "let down the bed wherein the sick of the palsy lay." One can visualize those immediately around Jesus helping to steady the bed as it came through the roof and was lowered to the floor. The four had accomplished their goal.

The scriptures do not record that the man with the palsy said anything. Perhaps after entering the house in such a spectacular manner, he was, for the moment, left without speech. But Jesus did not need to have him voice his request. His determination and ingenuity showed that he wanted to be healed. Jesus recognized his faith immediately. Although it is not mentioned specifically, the man with the palsy and those that bore him obviously believed that Jesus could cure him. Even more, they believed that he *would* cure him. Why else go to such an extent to bring him to Jesus? They were rewarded for their faith: the man was cured of both his physical and his spiritual impairments.

As the cure was effected the man's story ended, and the teaching surrounding the miracle began. Jesus had recognized the man's desire and had granted it. But this was not just another miracle. He perceived the thoughts of others in attendance and determined that the healing of this man could be an object lesson for the Pharisees, scribes, and doctors of the law who were watching. He would prove to them again that he was the Son of God.

Without any word from the sick man Jesus said, "Son, thy sins be forgiven thee." The statement was delivered with authority. The words were not a request but a declaration. Immediately the learned and the rulers of the Jews thought and reasoned in their hearts that he had blasphemed. To them, Jesus had usurped the very attributes that they reserved for God alone.

Their law prescribed no form for giving absolution from sin, for God alone held that power.[9] In their minds Jesus had made a "proclamation of His own sinlessness, and of His kingly dignity as the Messiah."[10] They did not openly acknowledge this, but they must have understood.

Jesus "perceived in his spirit" their reasoning. "Why reason ye these things in your hearts?" he asked them, thus deliberately placing before them his claim. He was the Messiah, and they now had the opportunity to either accept or reject him.

However, the rulers had long since developed ways of getting around the spiritual law in favor of their own needs, and they attempted to do so here. They did not answer at all, but remained silent. Jesus' question had been in response to their thoughts. They undoubtedly continued to reason mentally, perhaps thinking that although to forgive sins was blasphemy, to merely declare forgiveness of sins did not necessarily make it so. In their minds Jesus had sinned gravely, but he had given a "safe" declaration. He could declare the forgiveness of sins, but could not prove that they had been forgiven.

That Christ's enemies so reasoned is not recorded in the scripture, but Jesus' response indicates its probability. He posed another question, answering again their perceived thoughts. "Is it easier to say to the sick of the palsy, Thy sins be forgiven thee; or to say, Arise, and take up thy bed, and walk?" Jesus would now confirm that he could forgive sins: "But that ye may know that the Son of man hath power on earth to forgive sins, . . . I say unto thee, Arise, and take up thy bed." The sick man responded in the only way he could: "he arose, took up the bed, and went forth before them all." The bed that had been the sign of his disease was now the sign of his cure, and the proof that Jesus was the Messiah.

The Lord's procedure was deliberate. By first forgiving the palsied man's sins and then performing the miracle, he sealed his claim to Godhood. He had the power to forgive sins, for the miracle proved it. His relationship with the Father was exactly as he had represented it—he was the Son of God.

The procedure also implied a relationship between sin and bodily affliction. But all indications point to the Savior's witness to his Messiahship as being the primary purpose of this miracle. That the man wanted to be both spiritually and physically healed may be deduced from Matthew's record. Perhaps, to the man, the sins that tormented his mind were inseparably connected with the disease of his body. Whether they had actually caused the disease or whether the disease was the result of or punishment for sin is left to conjecture.

With this miracle Jesus demonstrated his power to forgive sin and he offered irrefutable proof that he was the Messiah. Despite this, the Jewish leaders, before whom the miracle was performed, refused to believe and chose to be blind to the obvious.

The One Born Blind

John 9:1–41

1. And as Jesus passed by, he saw a man which was blind from his birth.

2. And his disciples asked him, saying, Master, who did sin, this man, or his parents, that he was born blind?

3. Jesus answered, Neither hath this man sinned, nor his parents: but that the works of God should be made manifest in him.

4. I must work the works of him that sent me, while it is day: the night cometh, when no man can work.

5. As long as I am in the world, I am the light of the world.

6. When he had thus spoken, he spat on the ground, and made clay of the spittle, and he anointed the eyes of the blind man with the clay,

7. And said unto him, Go, wash in the pool of Siloam, (which is by interpretation, Sent.) He went his way therefore, and washed, and came seeing.

8. The neighbours therefore, and they which before had seen him that he was blind, said, Is not this he that sat and begged?

9. Some said, This is he: others said, He is like him: but he said, I am he.

10. Therefore said they unto him, How were thine eyes opened?

11. He answered and

said, A man that is called Jesus made clay, and anointed mine eyes, and said unto me, Go to the pool of Siloam, and wash: and I went and washed, and I received sight.

12. Then said they unto him, Where is he? He said, I know not.

13. They brought to the Pharisees him that aforetime was blind.

14. And it was the sabbath day when Jesus made the clay, and opened his eyes.

15. Then again the Pharisees also asked him how he had received his sight. He said unto them, He put clay upon mine eyes, and I washed, and do see.

16. Therefore said some of the Pharisees, This man is not of God, because he keepeth not the sabbath day. Others said, How can a man that is a sinner do such miracles? And there was a division among them.

17. They say unto the blind man again, What sayest thou of him, that he hath opened thine eyes? He said, He is a prophet.

18. But the Jews did not believe concerning him, that he had been blind, and received his sight, until they called the parents of him that had received his sight.

19. And they asked them, saying, Is this your son, who ye say was born blind? how then doth he now see?

20. His parents answered them and said, We know that this is our son, and that he was born blind:

21. But by what means he now seeth, we know not; or who hath opened his eyes, we know not: he is of age; ask him: he shall speak for himself.

22. These words spake his parents, because they feared the Jews: for the Jews had agreed already, that if any man did confess that he was Christ, he should be put out of the synagogue.

23. Therefore said his parents, He is of age; ask him.

24. Then again called they the man that was blind, and said unto him, Give God the praise: we know that this man is a sinner.

25. He answered and said, Whether he be a sinner or no, I know not: one thing I know, that, whereas I was blind, now I see.

26. Then said they to him again, What did he to thee? how opened he thine eyes?

27. He answered them, I have told you already, and ye did not hear: wherefore

would ye hear it again? will ye also be his disciples?

28. Then they reviled him, and said, Thou art his disciple; but we are Moses' disciples.

29. We know that God spake unto Moses: as for this fellow, we know not from whence he is.

30. The man answered and said unto them, Why herein is a marvellous thing, that ye know not from whence he is, and yet he hath opened mine eyes.

31. Now we know that God heareth not sinners: but if any man be a worshipper of God, and doeth his will, him he heareth.

32. Since the world began was it not heard that any man opened the eyes of one that was born blind.

33. If this man were not of God, he could do nothing.

34. They answered and said unto him, Thou wast altogether born in sins, and dost thou teach us? And they cast him out.

35. Jesus heard that they had cast him out; and when he had found him, he said unto him, Dost thou believe on the Son of God?

36. He answered and said, Who is he, Lord, that I might believe on him?

37. And Jesus said unto him, Thou hast both seen him, and it is he that talketh with thee.

38. And he said, Lord, I believe. And he worshipped him.

39. And Jesus said, For judgment I am come into this world, that they which see not might see; and that they which see might be made blind.

40. And some of the Pharisees which were with him heard these words, and said unto him, Are we blind also?

41. Jesus said unto them, If ye were blind, ye should have no sin: but now ye say, We see; therefore your sin remaineth.

Cross-reference:

JST John 9:4, 32

This is the final miracle of this series. In some respects the miracle is a combination of the previous two. For the rulers, it encompassed all the difficulties of Jesus' healing the one sick of the palsy and the explicitness of his healing the impotent man at the pool. The miracle occurred in Jerusalem after the Feast of Tabernacles. Jesus sent his disciples to the feast a day before he arrived and he went up to the feast "not openly, but as it were in secret" (see John 7:10). Jesus taught in the temple during the last two days of the feast. The discourses he taught served as a prelude to this miracle and assist in its explanation.

In John, chapters 5 and 7, Jesus teaches of his relationship with the Father; his "Light of the World" discourse is found in chapter 8. This miracle offered proof for the claims in the discourses. It would be hard to find a single, more complete miracle coupled with his discourses than this. The miracle contains—

1. All of the elements of Jesus' previous claims to the Messiahship.
2. The dilemma concerning the acceptance or rejection of his claims.
3. The foreshadowing of his future witness specifically aimed at the Sabbath law (see chapter 6).

Although these are secondary, it also contains—

4. A reference to the sin-disease-punishment problem.
5. The first open declaration in defense of Jesus before the Jewish leadership.

Jesus had preached for several days at the feast in Jerusalem. His discourses had openly proclaimed him as the Messiah. He may have performed other miracles during this stay in Jerusalem, but John recorded only this one.

Jesus and his disciples were walking in the city when they saw a beggar. The scripture seems to indicate that the man was well known, and he probably sat daily at this same spot. Justifiably a beggar because he was blind, he would sit and beg daily for his living, receiving from those who passed by as was required of them to give.[11] This was a Sabbath. The man could not openly beg on this day but could only sit and receive of the kindness of others as they passed and observed his condition.

As they passed, the disciples posed the first of several interesting questions raised by this miracle. They asked Jesus, "Master, who did sin, this man, or his parents, that he was born blind?" Much speculation has arisen from this question. Although the sin-disease-punishment (including physical disabilities and handicaps) relationship has been mentioned in previous miracles, we will now consider it in greater detail.

The controversy arising from this question raises several possibilities, but at least four should be considered:

1. That the offspring himself could commit some transgression that would cause the malady to be present from birth. Obviously this would have to be committed prior to birth.

2. That a sin or sins could be committed by the parents that would cause the offspring to suffer some malady.

3. That neither of the above two situations is applicable, but that God's divine plan is involved in some way which may or may not be known to us, and this is the cause of the malady. (Apparently this was the explanation in the case being considered.)

4. That normal and natural consequences of life—the result of man coming to and living upon the earth—may affect man to the extent of producing diseases, disabilities, and handicaps.

Let us discuss each of these possibilities in relation to the scriptural text:

1. *That the sin of the unborn offspring caused his disease or disability.* The first part of the question seems to indicate that the disciples had some knowledge of pre-earth existence; however, the extent of their knowledge is unknown. The idea that an unborn soul could have sinned may have evolved from existing Jewish teachings and customs. For example, the story of Jacob and Esau in the Old Testament was sometimes used to justify the commonly held belief that a child could commit sin before his birth.[12]

The Jews gave no accurate teachings on this matter at the time of Jesus. Therefore, the question posed by the disciples probably resulted from the current incorrect teachings. However, if Jesus had already instructed them on the pre-earth life doctrine, then they may have been requesting clarification on this particular man's circumstances.

There is no question that in the premortal state each individual was capable of obeying or disobeying God's commandments. We know that one-third of the children of God rebelled and were forever punished for this; as a result of that disobedience they could have no physical bodies, and will end up with Satan in outer darkness forever (see chapter 1). This example seemingly verifies that premortal obedience or disobedience may have consequences upon each person's subsequent existence. The problem is to determine situations in which these consequences occur.

2. *The sins of the parents could cause disease or disability in the child.* To best explain the ancient Jewish view on this matter, I quote the following (the words are couched as if from the mouth of God himself): "The good man, if prosperous, was so as the son of a righteous man; while the unfortunate good man suffered as the son of a sinful parent. So, also, the wicked man might be prosperous, if the son of a goodly parent; but if unfortunate, it showed that his parents had been sinners."[13]

The Jews were trained to regard special suffering as necessary or consequential to special sin.[14] Through apostate deviation they determined many situations as consequential to undisclosed or known sin. For example, "up to thirteen years of age a child was considered, as it were, part of his father, and as suffering for his guilt. More than that, the thoughts of a mother might affect the moral state of her unborn offspring, and the terrible apostasy of one of the greatest rabbis had, in popular belief, been caused by the sinful delight his mother had taken when passing through an idol-grove. Lastly, certain special sins in the parents would result in specific diseases in their offspring, and one is mentioned as causing blindness in children."[15]

The question thus posed by the disciples could have been completely Jewish, based on the common view that the merits or demerits of the parent would appear in the children, so the children became the evidence whereby the parents could be judged.[16] The question would have been perfectly normal in Jesus' day, and the disciples may have suspected that the parents' sins could have caused the poor man's predicament. Like the first possibility, this too was rejected by Jesus in the case we are now considering.

Nevertheless, the fact that the actions of parents can cause physical consequences for their children is well documented, and a specific cause of a malady can upon occasion be assigned in these cases. For example, if a mother is involved in drug abuse and her child is born addicted, or if a mother is affected with venereal disease and her child is consequently born blind, the cause-effect relationship is clear. Spiritual violations of God's commandments can also cause consequences for the children, the sins of Noah's contemporaries being a case in point. While the children may suffer such consequences of parental sin, in God's plan the parents and not the children will be punished for that sin, for "men will be punished for their own sins, and not for Adam's [or anyone else's] transgression" (Second Article of Faith; see 2 Nephi 4:3—6; D&C 68:25).

3. *God's providence was the cause.* In connection with this miracle Jesus offered another alternative to the two possibilities raised by the question of the disciples. They had asked the question expecting an answer. They wanted the "why" of the circumstance, but their two proposed alternatives did not apply to this situation. The man had been born blind for a purpose: that through him the power of God might be made manifest to others. He had been born blind so that Jesus might heal him, thereby verifying and testifying to the Jews that he was their Messiah. But this reason was unknown to the man for the many years preceding this miracle. Clearly, only divine knowledge could correctly ascribe this reason to an individual malady.

4. *Normal and natural consequences of life.* While God does not decree every malady that each individual mortal is subjected to, the overall plan of salvation (the plan accepted by God's spirit children in the council prior to the earth's creation) included the circumstances that cause these different maladies. As the Creator, God could undoubtedly issue a decree and make all disease, disability, and handicaps disappear. Mortality, however, is by its very nature imperfect and problem oriented. In the plan, sadness is the opposite of happiness; evil contrasts with good; hot opposes cold; and certainly mortality is the opposite of immortality. Mortality implies decay and ultimately death. Within mortality are accidents caused by man's actions that may result in injury. Imperfection means that in the ordinary course of events mistakes will be made that produce unpleasant results. If all knowledge, all insight, and all reason were available to man, traceable patterns could be seen in the causes and results of his actions. In each occurrence would appear a sequence of "laws," placed by God in his plan of creation, that would trace each of

these occurrences to its ultimate reason or source. This principle is basic to modern science and medicine, and by its implementation some diseases, disabilities, and handicaps have been overcome by man. Undoubtedly others will be in the future, for the potential is always there.

In the final analysis it seems that most diseases, physical disabilities, and handicaps are the result of natural and normal consequences rather than a punishment for sin. We may conclude this partly from Luke 13:1—5. Apparently some Galileans had been slain by Roman soldiers at the altar while sacrifices were being offered, and in telling Jesus of this tragic event those stating it assumed it was caused by the victims' sinfulness. Jesus specifically responded to this: "Suppose ye that these Galileans were sinners above all the Galileans, because they suffered such things? I tell you, Nay." He then added another historical example his listeners were familiar with. "Or those eighteen, upon whom the tower in Siloam fell, and slew them, think ye that they were sinners above all men that dwelt in Jerusalem?" Again he answered, "I tell you, Nay." Frequently such life occurrences are beyond any given individual's control and occur as a natural consequence of mortality. Because they are beyond any mortal's control, it is a miracle when one of them is prevented or corrected by the power of God.

These life-limiting and disabling conditions may or may not be caused by sin, and we should not attribute them either to God's will or to the breaking of his laws. It was the centuries-old apostasy of the Jews that caused them to think in this way.

The sin-punishment question has been discussed here in detail because of the obvious questions raised by the disciples' query to Jesus and the inferences drawn from other miracles. This question, however, was not the reason for the miracle. In fact, it was nothing more than a by-product of the historical treatment that has been given this miracle. The question of imputed sin as a reason for the blindness was inconsequential, and was treated as such by Jesus. He merely stated that neither the man nor his parents had sinned. He then proceeded to the miracle itself, the benefit the man received, and more significantly, the witness of his divinity.

Jesus "spat" upon the ground, made clay, and anointed the eyes of the blind man. Then he told him to go to the pool of Siloam and wash his eyes; and when he had done so, he "came seeing." The miracle was simple; the witness, more complex. This was a very public miracle, performed on the Sabbath and in a unique way.

Much has been written concerning Jesus' method of effecting the cure. He did not need the spittle or the clay. He did not need to anoint the eyes nor to have the man wash in the pool. Further, the cure had nothing to do with the Jewish teaching and belief in their primitive medicinal application of saliva (especially saliva from one fasting) to aid irritation and diseases of the eye.[17] All of these procedures were superfluous to the healing. So why did he do it?

Consider two possible reasons. The first involves the blind man himself. No indication is given that he knew or had even heard of Jesus before the miracle. He apparently learned the Lord's name at some time, for when he was questioned after the restoration of his sight he knew Jesus' name and disclosed this to the Pharisees, but he did not know his whereabouts. The value of Jesus' procedure in this case was found in the increase of the blind man's faith. The physical use of the clay on his sightless eyes may have somehow strengthened his belief in Christ, but it was not the clay that cured him. After the inquisition of the man was complete and he had been excommunicated, Jesus sought him out and asked, "Dost thou believe on the Son of God?" The man, confessing he did not know who the Son of God was, asked, "Who is he, Lord, that I might believe on him?" When Jesus told him it was He, the man worshipped him. The private benefits of this miracle were now complete for the blind man, resulting in both his physical healing and his spiritual growth.

The second possible reason for the Lord's unique method of healing exposes and illustrates the principal purpose of the miracle. Therein is contained two significant teachings, the first of which is symbolic. The blind man seemingly represented blind Israel; Jesus was the light of the world. The blind man had been given a set of instructions to follow. He followed these instructions completely, and his vision was restored. This simple relationship between the Lord's instructions and the obedience that produces the blessings brings to mind the Old Testament story of Elisha and Naaman. Naaman was told exactly what to do to be cleansed of his leprosy. At first he did not want to do it, but a servant reminded him of his desire to be clean. He then did as he had been instructed, and was healed (see 2 Kings 5:1—14).

Jesus had told Israel's rulers exactly who he was and how they could prove his claim. The rulers recognized Jesus' claim as the Messiah and knew the procedure necessary to prove him. All they had to do to receive a witness was follow this procedure, but they refused; that awful, willful blindness of those who will not see controlled their action.

The second teaching revolves around the Sabbath day and how it was observed by the rulers. Jesus made clay, anointed the eyes of the blind man, and instructed him to go and wash in the pool, thus deliberately breaking the Sabbath law that had been established by Israel's rulers. He had confronted the leaders with his claims earlier when he had healed the impotent man and had openly asserted his Messiahship. When he healed the man with the palsy, he placed them in a position of either accepting or rejecting him, and they remained silent, attempting to avoid the confrontation. But in this miracle his challenge and position was clear. He once more protested the strictness of the rabbinical observance of the law (which totally destroyed its true significance), thereby proclaiming himself Lord of the Sabbath. They knew that he had performed the miracle. They could no longer remain silent.[18]

By breaking their Sabbath law, Jesus opened himself to a charge that could be sustained against him. His teachings during the previous days also led to the inevitable conclusion that he was claiming to be the Messiah. But the Jewish leadership was in a dilemma. If they pressed the Sabbath-breaking charge, they would have to admit the validity of the miracle. If they admitted the miracle, they could not portray Christ as the criminal they wanted him to be.

Their predicament was such that even this unlearned and now healed blind man could confound them. They just could not overcome the fact that Jesus was right and they were wrong. Obviously a miracle had occurred, but they still attempted to discredit it. They first questioned the man and then his parents. They firmly established that he had been blind from birth and could now see. He who was blind called his benefactor a "prophet," but not even this status could be acknowledged by the rulers. Prophets could, under their law, set aside the Sabbath law, and they wanted Jesus to be a violator of the law. If they would not accept him, there was only one thing left for them to do: they must discredit him.

To the blind man the Pharisees accused Jesus. First, they said that he was not from God because he had broken the Sabbath. Second, they declared that he was a sinner. Finally, they boasted that they were Moses' disciples and that they knew "that God spake unto Moses: as for this fellow, we know not from whence he is."

But the recently healed man would not allow this. "Why herein is a marvellous thing," he began, "that ye know not from whence he is, and yet he hath opened mine eyes. Now we know that God heareth not sinners: but if any man be a worshipper of God, and doeth his will, him he heareth. Since the world began was it not heard that any man opened the eyes of one that was born blind. If this man were not of God, he could do nothing."

At this irrefutable argument the leaders became enraged. "Dost thou teach us?" they railed at him, declaring that he was "altogether born in sins." Then they "cast him out." The right was before them; it had been placed in direct contrast with their error, yet they chose to keep the error. They could not succeed in refuting the miracle; they could not blemish the character of Jesus; they could not even refute the unlearned man. In their frustration, they excommunicated the man who had been blind. Jesus found him later in the temple and completed his spiritual healing so that he might be saved. And the man "worshipped him."

Jesus continued to teach, and declared that he had come into the world that "they which see not might see; and that they which see might be made blind." Some Pharisees that were with Jesus heard this and asked, "Are we blind also?" They understood the application. They were saying that they were not blind and could see. But Jesus responded, "If ye were blind, ye should have no sin: but now ye say, we see; therefore your sin remaineth."

Those that previously could not see but accepted the proffered light were saved. But those that said they could see and would not, still remained in sin. There are none so blind as those who will not see. The light of the world had come and they had refused him.

Summary

Through his sermons and discourses, Jesus evidenced his Messiahship to the Jews and their leaders; by healing the impotent man at the pool at Bethesda, the one sick of the palsy, and the man born blind, he irrefutably confirmed it. The three individuals healed by these miracles received great blessings, both physically and spiritually. They would not forget Jesus. But in the divine plan even the individuals and their healings were eclipsed. These miracles were signs—signs that Jesus was the Messiah. He proclaimed it by his word and sealed the proclamation with his power. In each instance the Jewish leaders could have proclaimed him their king, but they would not.

Centuries of apostasy and modification of the law had corrupted their concept of the Messiah. Christ's miracles placed the rulers of Israel at odds with the expected Savior. They must either reject their error and accept him, or reject him and continue in darkness. The light of the world had come to shine in the darkness, but the darkness would not accept it. "We be Abraham's seed," they cried. "We are Moses' disciples"; "as for this fellow, we know not from whence he is." In his sermons the Lord had promised the Jews, "Ye shall know the truth, and the truth shall make you free." But they chose enslavement.

An Appeal to the Law

The three miracles discussed in this chapter center on a single theme: that of the Lord openly confronting the bastion of Jewish traditionalism, the Sabbath Law.

Jesus came to his chosen people to claim his rightful place as their Messiah, but the religion they practiced had changed significantly from that of old. Four hundred years had passed since the last of the Old Testament prophets. In the ensuing time the rabbinical rulers had risen to power. As the Jewish religion evolved without divine prophetic instruction, its principal hold upon the people was "the Law."

There is no way to determine just when the rabbis came into existence. They had developed gradually, probably beginning around the time of Ezra and Nehemiah.[1] Ezra is described as a "ready scribe," one who "had prepared his heart to seek the law of the Lord, and to do it, and to teach in Israel statutes and judgments (Ezra 7:6, 10). The Law of Moses had been altered, lost, or destroyed in the Diaspora and the destruction sustained through numerous wars. From Ezra's efforts and the efforts of others who had similar intent but less divine instruction developed the traditional law that governed the Jews when Jesus came.

At the time of Jesus the traditional law was divided into three sections. The first dictated scriptural investigation and contained the ordinances found in the written law. These included eternal laws delivered by Moses. Second was that which was to be observed. This was the "oral law" or the traditional teaching, and was implied in or deduced from the law of Moses. Third was the oral teaching in the broadest sense. This was "the hedge" placed around the Law by the Rabbis "to prevent any breach of the Law or customs, to ensure their exact observance, or to meet particular circumstances or dangers." It constituted the "sayings of the Scribes, or of the Rabbis," and traditionally was emphasized more than the written law and canonized each activity of life.[2]

The stronghold of this daily prescription was the Sabbath Law. "Nothing in Judaism had been left unfixed; every religious act, and indeed every act whatsoever, must follow intimately prescribed laws."[3] Jesus selected one particular element of the Sabbath Law to openly challenge—"doing good" on the Sabbath.

To heal on the Sabbath was strictly forbidden, except to save a life. The Jews had developed intricate procedures for giving medical aid on the Sabbath, and "their fine-spun casuistry had elaborate endless rules for the treatment of all maladies on the sacred day."[4] The Sabbath rules had grown into a law controlling all laws. The daily prescribed laws governing Jewish activities were reemphasized in stricter terms on the Sabbath.

An example of the complexity of Sabbath worship, specifically as it applied to health and sickness, follows:

> We have already seen, that in their view only actual danger to life warranted a breach of the Sabbath-Law. But this opened a large field for discussion. Thus, according to some, disease of the ear, according to some throat-disease, while, according to others, such a disease as angina, involved danger, and superseded the Sabbath-Law. All applications to the outside of the body were forbidden on the Sabbath. As regarded internal remedies, such substances as were used in health, but had also a remedial effect, might be taken, although here also there was a way of evading the Law. A person suffering from toothache might not gargle his mouth with vinegar, but he might use an ordinary toothbrush and

dip in vinegar. The Gemara [a book of the Law] here adds, that gargling was lawful, if the substance was afterwards swallowed. It further explains, that afflictions extending from the lips, or else from the throat, inwards, may be attended to, being regarded as dangerous. Quite a number of these are enumerated, showing, that either the Rabbis were very lax in applying their canon about mortal diseases, or else that they reckoned in their number not a few which we would not regard as such. External lesions also might be attended to, if they involved danger of life. Similarly, medical aid might be called in, if a person had swallowed a piece of glass; a splinter might be removed from the eye, and even a thorn from the body.[5]

Such was the Sabbath at the time of Christ. Concerning this, Jesus instructed his disciples:

> For they bind heavy burdens and grievous to be borne, and lay them on men's shoulders; but they themselves will not move them with one of their fingers.
> But all their works they do for to be seen of men: they make broad their phylacteries, and enlarge the borders of their garments,
> And love the uppermost rooms at feasts, and the chief seats in the synagogues,
> And greetings in the markets, and to be called of men, Rabbi, Rabbi.
> But be not ye called Rabbi: for one is your Master, even Christ; and all ye are brethren. (Matthew 23:4—8.)

The Lord directly confronted the Law in these three miracles because it was the foundation of Judaism at his time. He, as Jehovah in the Old Testament, had declared the sacredness of the Sabbath day. But the Jews had made of it a mockery. "The sabbath was made for man, and not man for the sabbath," Jesus declared. He was "Lord also of the sabbath." (Mark 2:27—28.)

This declaration concerning the Sabbath resulted from an act of his disciples on the Sabbath. The group was traveling, passing through cornfields as they went. The disciples began "to pluck the ears of corn" (Mark 2:23), "and to eat" (Matthew 12:1), a lawful act under the Law of Moses (see Deuteronomy 23:25).[6] Luke adds that the disciples "rubbed" the corn in their hands to separate the kernel from the husk (see Luke 6:1). This was considered "thrashing" and thus was unlawful on the Jewish Sabbath. When the Pharisees saw it (for they constantly watched Jesus to accuse, discredit, or destroy him), they challenged Jesus, saying, "Behold, thy disciples do that which is not lawful to do upon the sabbath day" (Matthew 12:2).

The inquiry, presented as a statement in Matthew and as a question in Mark and Luke, attempted to place Jesus at odds with the Law or his disciples. The cunning of it reflects the Pharisees' continuous attempt to entrap Jesus; for, in their minds, he would either be forced to confess that his disciples had transgressed the law, or he would have to defend his disciples in their purported transgression.

But Jesus would take neither position. Instead, he justified his disciples' actions as being exempt from the Law, and presented two examples to clearly vindicate them. The first example was of David and the shewbread (see 1 Samuel 21:1–6). At one time David and his men had eaten the sacred temple bread and were justified because of their extreme need.

The Lord's second example was even more relevant. The priests involved in the Levitical service did not cease from their work upon the Sabbath. Yet the Pharisees considered them blameless because the work was done in the temple. Lest his accusers resist this example with the argument that he and his disciples were not temple workers, Jesus added, "In this place is one greater than the temple" (Matthew 12:6). Thus his disciples were blameless, as were the priests and David, for the needs of their circumstance transcended the Law.

The Jews had made the Sabbath a day of prescribed activity that men observed only in form. The people were obsessed, avoiding transgressions with justified exactness. Likewise, the rulers defined with exactness the slightest potential transgression.

Christ's instructions on the Jewish Sabbath law might well be broadened to include all of their dull, mechanical obedience to every form of the Law. All of God's Law was made for man, not man for the Law. God's Law culminated in man's salvation. Man, in return, was to live the Law out of love for the giver of the Law, not just outwardly observe the Law for the Law's sake. The Law, after all, had been given to prepare Israel for the Messiah. But it had become the end instead of the means. The Jews had turned their devotion to the Law itself, and away from its giver.

Through the following three miracles Jesus declared the "spirit" as well as the "letter" of the Law. It was the gospel versus the Law as changed by rabbinic embellishment; Christ versus the rabbis. The gospel required a change of heart (see Alma 5). The Law required constant instruction, refinement, and arbitration on technical points. The gospel required that each action be made out of charity—the pure love of Christ. Under the Law, each act was to be in strict accordance with specific legal forms. Every detail of Jewish religious observance was prescribed and rigidly followed from the cradle to the grave.[7] In the gospel, man's action was testified to, confirmed, and comforted by the Holy Ghost. Under the Law, man's inactions (or disobedience) were punished by the court's ostracizing him from the community. Judgment, mercy, and faith, "the weightier matters of the law," had been eliminated (see Matthew 23:23).

"If ye continue in my word, then are ye my disciples indeed," Jesus said. "And ye shall know the truth, and the truth shall make you free." (John 8:31—32.) The truth would free the Jews from the over-legalized Law, and would allow them to overcome temptations and worldliness and accept Jesus for what he was—the Messiah.

Jesus confronted the Law to give another witness of his Messiahship. This witness was the result of each of these three miracles—the healing of the one with a withered hand, the woman with a spirit of infirmity, and the man with the dropsy.

The One with a Withered Hand

Mark 3:1—6

1. And he entered again into the synagogue; and there was a man there which had a withered hand.

2. And they watched him, whether he would heal him on the sabbath day; that they might accuse him.

3. And he saith unto the man which had the withered hand, Stand forth.

4. And he saith unto

them, Is it lawful to do good on the sabbath days, or to do evil? to save life, or to kill? But they held their peace.

5. And when he had looked round about on them with anger, being grieved for the hardness of their hearts, he saith unto the man,

Stretch forth thine hand. And he stretched it out: and his hand was restored whole as the other.

6. And the Pharisees went forth, and straightway took counsel with the Herodians against him, how they might destroy him.

Cross-references:

Matthew 12:9—14   Luke 6:6—11

This miracle is recorded by all three of the Synoptics. A minor discrepancy between Matthew's record and that of the other two concerns the question, "Is it lawful to do good on the sabbath days, or to do evil?" Matthew records that the rulers asked the question, while Mark and Luke record that Jesus did. Resolution of this minor conflict would seem possible, for Luke records that Jesus "knew their thoughts." It is probable then that Matthew, who usually condensed the record, merely combined the question—which was in the minds of the Pharisees and scribes and perceived by Jesus—with the actual asking of the question itself. But either way the result and purpose of the miracle are unaffected.

Jesus' performance of this miracle intentionally revealed the shallowness of the Law. The Pharisees were "watching him" to see if he would heal the man on the Sabbath. The man's life was not in immediate danger, so such a healing would violate their law.[8] The man was seated in the congregation in the synagogue. Whether brought there by the Pharisees or by happenstance is not recorded.

The man with the withered hand did not request to be healed (which would have been contrary to the Sabbath Law).[9] Jesus called for the man to "stand forth." After perceiving the thoughts of the Pharisees and scribes, he presented a question to the learned men. "Is it lawful to do good on the sabbath days, or to do evil? to save life, or to kill?" His question presented the basis for the miracle. Judaic law dictated that even doing good must be left to other days if it violated the rules of the Sabbath. The Lord's question postulated that if you failed to do good on the Sabbath, especially when the opportunity was specifically presented to you, then you had done evil. Thus the question made doing good not only allowable but a duty. The cunning, watchful Pharisees and scribes resorted to silence. For to answer no would condemn them and their law. To say yes would approve of what they must have known was about to happen. Again Jesus had placed them in an inextricable position.

Jesus looked "about on them with anger, being grieved for the hardness of their hearts." He told the man to stretch forth his hand; when he did, it "was restored whole as the other." Nothing else is said of the man, which suggests that he was neither the culprit of a plot nor the sole end of the miracle. He was the physical means Jesus used to declare his witness against the Law. Jesus had proclaimed himself "Lord also of the sabbath." The question and the miracle verified him as such. Again they must accept or reject him; there was no alternative. But their "law" was now the very obstacle between them and their Messiah. They remained silent, shut their eyes against the truth, and "went forth, and straightway took counsel with the Herodians against him, how they might destroy him."

Christ had broken Jewish tradition and put the Pharisees and scribes to open shame.

The Woman with a Spirit of Infirmity

Luke 13:10–17

10. And he was teaching in one of the synagogues on the sabbath.

11. And, behold, there was a woman which had a spirit of infirmity eighteen years, and was bowed together, and could in no wise lift up herself.

12. And when Jesus saw her, he called her to him, and said unto her, Woman, thou art loosed from thine infirmity.

13. And he laid his hands on her: and immediately she was made straight, and glorified God.

14. And the ruler of the synagogue answered with

indignation, because that Jesus had healed on the sabbath day, and said unto the people, There are six days in which men ought to work: in them therefore come and be healed, and not on the sabbath day.

15. The Lord then answered him, and said, Thou hypocrite, doth not each one of you on the sabbath loose his ox or his ass from the stall, and lead him away to watering?

16. And ought not this woman, being a daughter of Abraham, whom Satan hath bound, lo, these eighteen years, be loosed from this bond on the sabbath day?

17. And when he had said these things, all his adversaries were ashamed: and all the people rejoiced for all the glorious things that were done by him.

This miracle indicated with power and testimony Christ's position on the Sabbath day issue. Jesus was teaching in the synagogue on the Sabbath. A woman was present that had "a spirit of infirmity eighteen years." She was bent over and could not straighten herself. She did not request the miracle, but her presence in the synagogue might indicate her personal hope for the Lord's help. Jesus called her to him and told her that she was loosed from her infirmity. He then laid his hands upon her to perform the miracle. Jesus seldom used this method, but perhaps did so here to assist the faith of the woman and to instruct the disciples in the method that later they would use and apply with the priesthood (see James 5:14–15; D&C 42:44).

That the woman needed both physical and spiritual healing is evident from the words of Jesus. She was "loosed" from her infirmity, and he said Satan had bound her "these eighteen years."

Again, the Lord would do "good" on the Sabbath. In the case of the one with the withered hand, the Lord communicated his intentions before the miracle; here the miracle was performed and his counsel followed. After the miracle had taken place, the ruler of the synagogue upbraided the congregation. He was incensed at the "Sabbath breaking," and expressed the thoughts and conclusions of the Pharisees concerning Christ's actions on the Sabbath. "There are six days in which men ought to work," he stated. "In them therefore come and be healed, and not on the sabbath day." What the Pharisees and scribes at the healing of the one with the withered hand would not say, this ruler openly and angrily put forth. Although apparently berating the congregation as a whole, it was obvious that his comments were directed to the woman and Jesus. Although the woman (perhaps a member of his congregation)[10] had received a great blessing, he could see only an irregularity, a departure from the normal Sabbath worship. He cared not for her healing; he was cold and bound by tradition, a rabbinical pedant.

Jesus again openly confronted the Law as he denounced the ruler's empty formalism. Unusually severe, he responded, "Thou hypocrite, doth not each one of you on the sabbath loose his ox or his ass from the stall, and lead him away to watering?" This was a "daughter of Abraham," he declared, "whom Satan hath bound, lo, these eighteen years." Surely this woman of the covenant should merit as much compassion as these dumb animals.

His adversaries were "ashamed" but unconverted. The people rejoiced, but still could not apply these teachings and recognize their long-awaited Messiah.

The Man with the Dropsy

Luke 14:1—6

1. And it came to pass, as he went into the house of one of the chief Pharisees to eat bread on the sabbath day, that they watched him.

2. And, behold, there was a certain man before him which had the dropsy.

3. And Jesus answering spake unto the lawyers and Pharisees, saying, Is it lawful to heal on the sabbath day?

4. And they held their peace. And he took him, and healed him, and let him go;

5. And answered them, saying, Which of you shall have an ass or an ox fallen into a pit, and will not straightway pull him out on the sabbath day?

6. And they could not answer him again to these things.

This last of three miracles directed at the Jewish Law was performed late in the ministry of Jesus. Its circumstances indicate that even at this late date Jesus had not given up offering the kingdom to the Pharisees. It also indicated that even though he again offered them the kingdom, they had so hardened their hearts against him that they would not see the obvious.

Jesus had been invited to the home of one of the chief Pharisees to partake of the Sabbath meal. At Jesus' time the rabbis often used the Sabbath day for social entertainment.[11] The invitation was not abnormal, but it concealed sinister intentions. Luke reports that they "watched him," and it appears that the sole purpose of the invitation was to lure him to do evil in their eyes.

A man with dropsy was present at the dinner. The scripture does not say whether he had been placed there specifically by the Pharisees to provoke Jesus to yet another healing on the Sabbath, or whether he came on his own. These meals were partly for charitable purposes, and the poor and the sick were permitted to come in uninvited and eat.[12] The man could have heard that Jesus was in the home and went, hoping that the Master would take notice of him and grant his desire.

Jesus brought the man before him and asked the Pharisees the same question he had asked before. "Is it lawful to heal on the sabbath day?" His purpose was still the same: he would place the kingdom of God and the Messiah in direct confrontation with the Law as the rulers dictated it. And as before they held their peace. There could be no alternative explanations or answers. Jesus had phrased his Sabbath question in such a manner that it left no such possibility. Rabbinical schools had arisen based on disputes over the Law. But to Jesus, the Law had been meant to lead people to the kingdom of heaven, and only one answer was possible. His question, if answered with a no, had to be answered before the guests, for the Pharisees were responsible to so instruct those present.[13] But since the answer was obviously yes, the leaders remained silent lest they in any manner seem to approve or accept Christ. They would not reject the law they held so dear.

Jesus healed the man and "let him go." Whether the man came hoping to be healed or had been invited (not knowing the purpose of the Pharisees) did not matter. He had received the blessing and was excused.

The "chief Pharisee," "perhaps a member of the Great Sanhedrin itself," and the other "prominent and influential"[14] guests, would now be chastened by the Messiah.

Jesus had been invited to dine with this group of self-aggrandizing leaders who, as was their tradition, scrambled for places at the table according to reputation and social status.[15] But he disapproved of this social custom. To aspire to the so-called honor of men was not important to him. To assist "the poor, the maimed, the lame, the blind" was important, "for whosoever exalteth himself shall be abased; and he that humbleth himself shall be exalted" (Luke 14:11—13).

The teaching example was over. The Jewish leaders could no more accept Christ now than they could earlier. He had given them testimony and example, specifically applied it to the Sabbath Law, and sealed it with a miracle to prove his authority. But still, "they held their peace."

Part Four

Jesus' Messiahship Witnessed to the Apostles

Selection and Call

The First Draught of Fish

Luke 5:1–11

1. And it came to pass, that, as the people pressed upon him to hear the word of God, he stood by the lake of Gennesaret,

2. And saw two ships standing by the lake: but the fishermen were gone out of them, and were washing their nets.

3. And he entered into one of the ships, which was Simon's, and prayed him that he would thrust out a little from the land. And he sat down, and taught the people out of the ship.

4. Now when he had left speaking, he said unto Simon, Launch out into the deep, and let down your nets for a draught.

5. And Simon answering said unto him, Master, we have toiled all the night, and have taken nothing: nevertheless at thy word I will let down the net.

6. And when they had this done, they inclosed a great multitude of fishes: and their net brake.

7. And they beckoned unto their partners, which were in the other ship, that they should come and help

them. And they came, and filled both the ships, so that they began to sink.

8. When Simon Peter saw it, he fell down at Jesus' knees, saying, Depart from me; for I am a sinful man, O Lord.

9. For he was astonished, and all that were with him, at the draught of the fishes which they had taken:

10. And so was also James, and John, the sons of Zebedee, which were partners with Simon. And Jesus said unto Simon, Fear not; from henceforth thou shalt catch men.

11. And when they had brought their ships to land, they forsook all, and followed him.

Cross-references:

Matthew 4:18—22   Mark 1:16—20

This part of the book contains the special miracles directed to the Twelve Apostles. Some were performed before their call, and some after. The miracles were a special witness by Jesus to them that he was the Messiah, the promised Savior of the world. These were the men who would live and travel with Jesus throughout his ministry. They were different from those disciples that followed him generally. They were to lead the Church and testify of him, that others might come to know and believe.

Then as now, a disciple was someone who elected to follow Jesus and generally believed on his word. These followers were devoted to him, but they did not receive the special witness of the Apostles. The Apostles did not volunteer for their calling. Luke reports that the Lord "continued all night in prayer to God" (Luke 6:12) prior to the selection of the first Twelve. Having selected and called these from his disciples in general, he ordained them to the Apostleship. He reminded them of this special calling in his last instructions to them, given just before his death. "Ye have not chosen me," he said, "but I have chosen you, and ordained you" (John 15:16). The call of Apostle is one reserved for the Melchizedek Priesthood, "comprising as a distinguishing function that of personal and special witness to the divinity of Jesus Christ as the one and only Redeemer and Savior of mankind."[1]

At the time of the miracle of the first draught of fish, four of these future, special witnesses were called to follow the Savior: Peter, his brother Andrew, James, and his brother John. Although the selection of the four is mentioned in all three of the synoptic Gospels, only Luke records the miracle.

The call to follow Jesus in his ministry was a sacred experience, and how each of these four men chose to report it may well be reflected in the accounts that have come down to us. While each of the three Synoptics recorded at least some portion of the event, John elected to remain silent about it, as he so often did when he was personally involved in close relationships with the Lord. From the detail that is recorded, it is evident that the experience was an extremely personal and impressive one, causing the deepest soul-searching and commitment.

How well these disciples had known Jesus or followed him prior to this call is not known. It should be evident from the text and circumstance of the miracle, however, that they certainly knew of him, and perhaps had even received personal witness of his divine mission.

Although he did not report the calling of the four, John indicates that they had had some association with Jesus before the miracle. He records that the day after the baptism of Jesus, John the Baptist and two of his disciples were standing as Jesus walked by, and the Baptist, true to his mission and call, testified, "Behold the Lamb of God" (John 1:36). The two disciples followed Jesus. The Lord asked them what they were doing, and they inquired where he was staying. Invited to come and see, they stayed with the Lord that day. John identifies one of these two as Andrew, Peter's brother. The other has always been thought to be John himself.

As the miracle develops, Luke reports that Jesus was teaching by the Lake of Gennesaret, one of his favorite teaching places. The crowd of people "pressed upon him" to hear the word of God. Two empty fishing ships stood by the shore. The fishermen were washing their nets nearby. The ships belonged to Peter, his brother Andrew, and James and John. Jesus went aboard Peter's boat and requested that Peter "thrust out a little from the land." This gained him some separation from the crowd, allowing the multitude to sit or stand on the shore, that all might see and hear him as he continued to teach "the people out of the ship." When he had finished the sermon he requested that Peter "launch out into the deep." Although Jesus had just taught of the kingdom of God from the deck of their boat, Peter and his partners were now to gain a much stronger testimony of him.

"Let down your nets for a draught," Jesus told Peter. The partners had been fishing all night, possibly in that very area, but had caught nothing. Peter told the Lord of this and continued, "Nevertheless at thy word I will let down the net."

Obviously Peter had confidence in the Lord. Perhaps hearing Christ's sermon had instilled this unquestionable belief, but more probably it was built upon Peter's previous acquaintance with the Lord. His confidence and faith had grown; thus, despite having labored all night in vain, when instructed to do so Peter let down the nets.

This simple act symbolized the Savior's plan for these four fishermen. He would later choose them from among all his disciples to become Apostles, and at least three of them would hold a special position in his eyes, even among the Twelve. Jesus drew these four fishermen to him just as the fishermen drew in the "multitude of fishes." They cast their nets in, and the catch was so great that the net broke. When they called to their partners, James and John, for help, they gladly came so that they, too, might participate in the catch. There were so many fish that when they took them into the ships, both were filled and began to sink. The future Apostles knew that they were in the presence of one greater than themselves.

Only Peter's reaction to the miracle is recorded. He fell "at Jesus' knees, saying, Depart from me; for I am a sinful man, O Lord." Peter and his brethren were frightened at the Lord's display of power. Peter's response was not a sign of weakness or unbelief, nor did Peter desire that the Lord should actually depart from him. Peter had merely expressed his own feelings of personal unworthiness at being in the Lord's presence.

The reaction was not unusual. Moses, Isaiah, Jeremiah, Gideon, Paul, and even John the Revelator, are recorded as acting much the same upon being called by the Lord to serve him (see Exodus 3:11; 4:10—17; Isaiah 6:5; Jeremiah 1:6; Judges 6:15;

Acts 9:6; Revelation 1:17). All these great men expressed their personal unworthiness, yet in no instance was weak faith implied. So it was with Peter. He did not feel worthy to stay in the presence of the Lord, but the Lord would not leave him; he had a great work for Peter and the others to do. In his response to Simon, Christ comforted him and said, "Fear not; from henceforth thou shalt catch men."

The fishermen recognized Christ's witness to them through the miracle, and they acknowledged it. The Psalmist had sung of him: "Thou madest him to have dominion over the works of thy hands; . . . the fowl of the air, and the fish of the sea (see Psalms 8:6, 8). Jesus' control over these creatures had received ample witness. He had spoken only to Peter to instruct him to let down his net, yet the "fish of the sea" had gathered that they might be drawn in. In so doing, Jesus had let down the gospel net, and had brought in four men who would be special witnesses of him. They would now be fishers of men, to bring all who would come into the kingdom of God. Finally, the record states that they brought their ship to shore and "forsook all, and followed him."

A rich man once asked Jesus how to gain eternal life. Jesus enumerated the basic commandments, to which the man openly acknowledged his compliance. The man continued his inquiry: "What lack I yet?" Jesus told him to sell all that he had, give the proceeds to the poor, and follow him. "But when the young man heard that saying, he went away sorrowful: for he had great possessions." (See Matthew 19:16–26).

Not so with the four fishermen. "They forsook all, and followed him." All that had meant so much to them—their boats, their nets and gear, their livelihood, and even their families—they left behind. These things had occupied their thoughts daily, but "from that moment the four were His devoted followers. The rich gain they would have prized so highly but an hour before, had lost its charm. Called to decide there and then, as a proof of their meekness for discipleship, they forsook all, and followed Him at once."[2]

Not all of the Twelve were present when this miracle occurred but they would eventually hear of it, for these humble fishermen would bear witness of it to them.

The Final Draught of Fish

John 21:1—10

1. After these things Jesus shewed himself again to the disciples at the sea of Tiberias; and on this wise shewed he himself.

2. There were together Simon Peter, and Thomas called Didymus, and Nathanael of Cana in Galilee, and the sons of Zebedee, and two other of his disciples.

3. Simon Peter saith unto them, I go a fishing. They say unto him, We also go with thee. They went forth, and entered into a ship immediately; and that night they caught nothing.

4. But when the morning was now come, Jesus stood on the shore: but the disciples knew not that it was Jesus.

5. Then Jesus saith unto them, Children have ye any meat? They answered him, No.

6. And he said unto them, Cast the net on the right side of the ship, and ye shall find. They cast therefore, and now they were not able to draw it for the multitude of fishes.

7. Therefore that disciple whom Jesus loved saith unto Peter, It is the Lord. Now when Simon Peter heard that it was the Lord, he girt his fisher's coat unto him, (for he was naked,) and did cast himself into the sea.

8. And the other disciples came in a little ship; (for they were not far from land, but as it were two hundred cubits,) dragging the net with fishes.

9. As soon then as they were come to land, they saw a fire of coals there, and fish laid thereon, and bread.

10. Jesus saith unto them, Bring of the fish which ye have now caught.

This miracle mirrors that of the first draught of fish. All its elements are basically the same. However, this final draught takes place after the resurrection of the Lord, but prior to his ascension.

The first draught of fish had instituted the call to four fishermen to follow Christ. Through their testimonies it extended to the other Apostles. The final draught of fish reaffirmed that call. Christ, through this "duplicate" miracle, seemingly confirmed and verified to the Apostles four specific things:

1. He was the Son of God, the Messiah—the resurrected Lord.

2. The Apostles had been called to Christ's ministry, and despite their actions at his trial and death, they were acceptable before him, except for Judas.

3. He had "chosen" them.

4. They would again completely yield themselves and all that they had to him and his service.

Interestingly, John did not record the first miracle at all, but he is the only gospel writer to record this one.

After his resurrection, Jesus had appeared to the Apostles at least twice prior to this appearance (see Luke 24:33—36; John 20:19, 26). He had told the Apostles to go into Galilee where he would show himself to them (see Matthew 28:10). They had done so. Not all of the group were present for this miracle. John records that he, Peter, James, Thomas, and Nathanael were present, plus two other "disciples" who are left unnamed. It has been assumed that the "two disciples" here referred to were also numbered among the Apostles.[3]

It would appear from the scriptures that the group had been in Galilee some time, perhaps several days, and they were impatient for the Lord's impending visit. Peter finally exclaimed, "I go a fishing." The others readily agreed, and all departed to the lake. The Apostles had just experienced several days of very unusual happenings. The Lord had been crucified and had risen from the tomb. He had appeared and taught them, and had performed many signs and wonders (see John 20:30). They would now relax the stress and tension of these days by fishing. Because they were in Galilee, they would use their own boats. In all probability this miracle occurred in the same location as that of the first draught.

The Apostles fished all night and caught nothing. As the morning broke, a figure appeared on the shore. It was Jesus, but the Apostles "knew not that it was Jesus" (see chapter 12). He did not want to be known to them at first. Jesus inquired, "Children, have ye any meat?" He knew that they had nothing, but he would have them remember the former miracle and the call to the work. They responded and answered no, still unaware that it was Jesus.

Jesus then told the Apostles to "cast the net on the right side of the ship," and they would find fish. The same setting now existed as in the miracle of the first draught of fish. The "unknown stranger" in that instance was the same as in this. He had been unknown to them as the Messiah then, and in a different sense was unknown as the Messiah now. Their faith and confidence in him had been sufficient at the first miracle to "let down the net," but now they did not recognize him as the Messiah. However, perhaps subconsciously recalling the earlier miracle, they cast the net on the right side of the boat. The Spirit was now moving upon them. "They cast therefore, and now they were not able to draw it for the multitude of fishes." When the stranger in the first draught was revealed, Peter knew and acknowledged him. In the second draught John said unto Peter, "It is the Lord."

The character of some of the Apostles is beautifully shown in the recording of this miracle. John, who was always reserved when it came to his relationship with Jesus, did not even record his own name. He recorded himself as one of the "sons of Zebedee" at the commencement of the miracle, and as "that disciple whom Jesus loved" when he recognized Christ.

Peter was so excited when he recognized the Lord that he grabbed his coat and "cast himself into the sea." He wanted to swim to shore and his Master. The "multitude of fish" was no more important to him now than in the earlier miracle. The others followed in a small boat, "dragging the net with fishes," but Peter's excitement and love for the Lord overcame his normal tendencies to share in such work.

Jesus had prepared a fire, and he now asked the men to bring him some fish. Peter returned to the net and helped drag it ashore. They then dined.

A curious comment is now recorded. As Jesus invited them to dine, none dared ask, "Who art thou?" for they knew "that it was the Lord." No one had been resurrected before; they wanted reassurance, yet in their hearts they knew. John now notes that it was the third time that the Lord had appeared to them.

After they had finished eating, Jesus instructed them and reaffirmed their call. Again the Lord addressed only Peter, as in the first draught of fish, although the charge obviously was applied to all of the Apostles. Referring to the fish, the Lord said, "Simon . . . lovest thou me more than these?" Even though differently phrased, the same question had been asked in the first draught, wherein the Lord said "Follow me" (Matthew 4:19).

To the question Peter responded, "Yea, Lord; thou knowest that I love thee." Twice more the Lord asked and twice more Peter answered. By the time the third inquiry came, "Peter was grieved." He undoubtedly remembered that dreadful night when three times he had denied that he knew the Lord.

Peter answered, "Lord, thou knowest all things; thou knowest that I love thee." Gone now was the previous fear in his heart for his personal safety. He stood before his Savior, knowing that Jesus knew his feelings and the reasons for his former denial. Peter openly confessed his love for Jesus. He was forgiven.

Soon blessed with the reception of the Holy Ghost (see Acts 2:2–4), Peter went on to become the chief Apostle, the earthly leader of the Church. He developed such strong faith that his reputation spread among the Saints, and "they brought forth the sick into the streets, and laid them on beds and couches, that at the least the shadow of Peter passing by might overshadow some of them" (Acts 5:15).

As in the first draught of fish, the Lord (now the resurrected Savior) extended his call to the Apostles, and they received a personal manifestation that he was the Messiah.

Signs and Powers 8

Stilling the Tempest

Mark 4:35–41

35. And the same day, when the even was come, he saith unto them, Let us pass over unto the other side.

36. And when they had sent away the multitude, they took him even as he was in the ship. And there were also with him other little ships.

37. And there arose a great storm of wind, and the waves beat into the ship, so that it was now full.

38. And he was in the hinder part of the ship, asleep on a pillow: and they awake him, and say unto him, Master, carest thou not that we perish?

39. And he arose, and rebuked the wind, and said unto the sea, Peace, be still. And the wind ceased, and there was a great calm.

40. And he said unto them, Why are ye so fearful? how is it that ye have no faith?

41. And they feared exceedingly, and said one to another, What manner of man is this, that even the wind and the sea obey him?

Cross-references:

Matthew 8:23—27   Luke 8:22—25   JST Luke 8:23

This chapter deals with four miracles directed to the Apostles to teach them further of Jesus and instruct them of his authority. As in all the miracles, the teaching is directed toward Jesus, and contains specific evidence that he is the Son of God. But in these miracles, the personal power of Jesus is revealed.

The stilling of the tempest, like walking on the water, is a miracle that might stretch one's faith in the miraculous. Over the centuries no miracles have created more consternation for those who would explain away the miraculous than these two miracles.[1] The Apostles' reaction to each of these remarkable miracles, however, testifies to their authenticity.

The stilling of the tempest cannot be explained by any known laws, and there are no natural theories that apply. To cast it out as fabrication brings suspicion on all of the miracles, and may destroy the validity of the entire scriptural text. It must either be believed or rejected, thereby causing acceptance or rejection of him who performed it.

All three Synoptics record the stilling of the tempest. They give divergent reports, but such divergence can be attributed to the individual impressions of the writers, expecially regarding the order of events surrounding the miracle. All the writers agree upon the descriptive circumstances of the miracle itself.

Jesus, possibly after a long and arduous day, had decided to "pass over unto the other side" of the Lake of Gennesaret. Mark emphasized that no particular preparation had been made for the trip, which provides a potential explanation for some of the teachings that Jesus had just delivered. As they embarked, several members of the multitude asked if they could accompany him. First was a scribe, to whom Jesus responded, "Foxes have holes, and the birds of the air have nests; but the Son of man hath not where to lay his head" (Matthew 8:20). Another asked to go, but indicated that he must first bury his dead father. The Lord responded, "Let the dead bury their dead" (Matthew 8:22).

These teachings are better understood if coupled with Christ's

instructions to depart immediately without making any prepara-
tions. To follow him meant to go at his command and to place
the needs of the kingdom above personal, worldly needs. Not
that one should literally have to leave immediately and force
others to bury a dead father to be required to wander homeless,
but that the requirements of the kingdom were more important
than worldly problems. These conflicts were always to be satisfied in favor of the kingdom of God, not of the mundane cares of
this life.[2]

As the ship left the shore the Lord found refreshment from his
weariness.[3] Physically exhausted, he fell asleep, and was still in
the rear of the ship asleep on a pillow when the storm arose on
the lake.

It was not unusual for storms to arise quickly on the Lake of
Gennesaret, and "a sudden and violent squall [arose], such as
these small inland seas, surrounded with mountain gorges, are
notoriously exposed to."[4] But this was no ordinary storm. The
wind was so great that "the waves beat into the ship, so that it
was now full." These men were sailors and fishermen and had
been out on the lake many times, yet this storm caused the boat
to become unmanageable. The waves were high, all but
swamping the boat. Through the darkness of the clouds, the
fierce wind, and the tumult and confusion of the storm, Jesus
slept.

Many hundreds of years before, a similar storm had raged in
the Mediterranean Sea. Jonah had been called of the Lord to go
to Nineveh to cry repentance and to warn them of impending
destruction should they not heed his call. Fearful for his own life,
he attempted to escape the Lord. He took passage on a ship
headed for Tarshish. But the "Lord sent out a great wind," and a
great tempest arose so that "the ship was like to be broken." Although all the mariners on the ship were terrified and feared
death, Jonah slept. Awakened by the sailors, he recognized the
perilous position the ship was in and acknowledged that he was
the cause. He suggested that they throw him overboard so that
the storm would cease. Hesitating for only a moment, the
anxious mariners gladly accepted the suggestion and obligingly
threw Jonah into the sea.

The balance of Jonah's story is well known and of no importance to this miracle, but the result of casting Jonah into the sea is. The scripture reports, "they took up Jonah, and cast him forth into the sea: and the sea ceased from her raging." (See Jonah 1:1–15.) As the Lord's requirements were fulfilled, the storm ceased.

Although both Jonah and the Lord slept through the tempest, they did so in different frames of mind. There was no peace in Jonah's heart, and the analogy ends with the calming of the tempest. But the Apostles would have known the story of Jonah from childhood and would have been taught the power of God over the elements. Now they were in like peril, and they awakened the Savior and cried, "Master, carest thou not that we perish?"

Jesus arose and rebuked the wind, "and said unto the sea, Peace, be still. And the wind ceased, and there was a great calm." His power over the elements was again revealed—his Messiahship witnessed. The elements obeyed Jesus because he was their Master. As the Creator, he had brought them into being on this earth, and they obeyed his will.

When Jehovah calmed the sea in Jonah's time, even the heathen mariners recognized his power (see Jonah 1:16). Now incarnate, Jehovah again displayed his power over the elements. This powerful authority Christ held was encompassed in the authority he endowed the Apostles with when he ordained them (see John 15:16).

During the storm the Apostles had sought the Lord's help to alleviate their immediate danger, and he did not leave them helpless. But in their seeking, the Lord found a teaching moment. He mildly rebuked them saying, "Why are ye so fearful? How is it that ye have no faith?" It was not that they did not have "any" faith, for their call to the Lord for help signified that they believed he could and would assist them. Their error had been in the great fear they had displayed—as if a storm would or could destroy the Son of God.[5] They also held his priesthood authority (see Mark 3:14), and through it they could have calmed the storm and alleviated their fears, but they were still learning.

The Apostles' response to this miracle is interesting. They were in awe of the Lord and asked, "What manner of man is this?" They understood his power—he had demonstrated that;

but they were still trying to understand the man. As did the people of Nazareth, perhaps they still looked upon him as a man, not yet as the Messiah.

This miracle also contains a symbolic teaching concerning the tempest within each soul. Isaiah said, "But the wicked are like the troubled sea, when it cannot rest, whose waters cast up mire and dirt. There is no peace, saith my God, to the wicked." (Isaiah 57:20—21; see also Jude 1:13.) As the Lord calmed the troubled sea, so will the troubled soul tossed by the tempest of a sinful world find peace in the Lord, and the resulting calm will testify of his power.[6]

The Psalmist sang, "O Lord God of hosts, who is a strong Lord like unto thee? or to thy faithfulness round about thee? Thou rulest the raging of the sea: when the waves thereof arise, thou stillest them." (Psalm 89:8—9.) The Apostles had gained greater insight into the Messiah. They had strengthened their testimony of him as the Son of God and had a greater understanding of the power that he had given them. But most of all, he had indelibly confirmed in their hearts that he was the Prince of Peace.

Walking on the Water

Matthew 14:24—33

24. But the ship was now in the midst of the sea, tossed with waves: for the wind was contrary.

25. And in the fourth watch of the night Jesus went unto them, walking on the sea.

26. And when the disciples saw him walking on the sea, they were troubled, saying, It is a spirit; and they cried out for fear.

27. But straightway Jesus spake unto them, saying, Be of good cheer; it is I; be not afraid.

28. And Peter answered him and said, Lord, if it be thou, bid me come unto thee on the water.

29. And he said, Come. And when Peter was come down out of the ship, he walked on the water, to go to Jesus.

30. But when he saw the wind boisterous, he was

afraid; and beginning to sink, he cried, saying, Lord, save me.

31. And immediately Jesus stretched forth his hand, and caught him, and said unto him, O thou of little faith, wherefore didst thou doubt?

32. And when they were come into the ship, the wind ceased.

33. Then they that were in the ship came and worshipped him, saying, Of a truth thou art the Son of God.

Cross-references:

Mark 6:47—51   John 6:16—21   JST Mark 6:50

This miracle is recorded in three of the four Gospels, but not the same three that recorded the stilling of the tempest. Luke does not record this miracle, whereas John does. The stories recounted by the three are very similar. As noted in the discussion on the stilling of the tempest, Jesus, as Jehovah, had placed on the earth the elements and the laws governing them that he was now miraculously "defying." There is no contradiction in this, for clearly the God who established the law can hold it in abeyance for his purposes.

All of the Gospel writers agree on the circumstances preceding the miracle. The feeding of the five thousand had just taken place. The events of that miracle, in which the Apostles were participants, were particularly Jewish in expectation of the Messiah (see chapter 2). Perhaps the Apostles were in danger of being caught up in the emotion and the worldly desires of the multitude. At any rate, Jesus "constrained" them to "get into a ship, and to go before him unto the other side" of the lake. He required them to leave "while he sent the multitudes away." Jesus then went to "a mountain" to pray. (See Matthew 14:22—23.) He stayed for some hours in the solitude he must have often desired but seldom obtained.

Meanwhile, the Apostles had taken the ship and left for the other side of the lake. They intended to cross over and wait for Jesus as he had instructed them to do, but "the wind was contrary." As they were "toiling in rowing," Jesus, still on the land, saw them. The ship was unmanageable, and he determined to go to their aid. They had been rowing for hours but had not progressed far, even though it was now the fourth watch, or between 3:00 A.M. and 6:00 A.M.[7] Jesus approached them, walking upon the water. The Apostles saw the Lord upon the water and were frightened, just as they had been at the stilling of the tempest. This was not a public miracle intended to receive the plaudits of a stricken and astonished multitude. This was the Messiah witnessing to his chosen Twelve that he was the Son of God, and reaffirming that he had total power over heaven and earth. This was he who had gathered together the waters and called them seas, and said that it was good (see Genesis 1:10).

Although the Lord had given authority to Moses to part the Red Sea (see Exodus 14:21—22), and to Elijah and Elisha (by use of the mantle) to part the Jordan River (see 2 Kings 2:8, 14), neither had walked on other than dry ground. Elisha also performed an interesting miracle involving the same principle that Jesus now exercised. The story would have been known to the Apostles. Elisha had gone with others to the banks of the Jordan River to cut timber. As one of the group "was felling a beam, the axe head fell into the water." The man expressed concern to Elisha, for the axe had been "borrowed." Elisha asked where it had entered into the river, and the man showed him the place. Elisha then cut a stick and "cast it in thither; and the iron did swim." The man took up the head, and it was restored to him. The story is unique, to say the least. Elisha used the power of the priesthood to locate the axe head, bring it to the surface of the river, and cause it to move toward the man that he might reclaim it. The head of the axe was iron, and therefore could not "float" of its own accord. But the power Elisha exercised caused it to "defy" the law of gravity and become buoyant, even mobile, that it might "swim" to him who lost it. (See 2 Kings 6:4—7.)

The same principle is used in this miracle. There is no natural law that can be quoted in an attempt to explain the miracle. Did Jesus' body become exempt from the law of gravity, or did the water become solid under his feet? We do not know. As in the case of the iron axe head, the normal laws became inoperative and a higher power replaced them. Seeing the Savior walking toward them on the water, the Apostles were frightened and "troubled," and they "cried out for fear." They thought he was "a spirit" or a ghost. They were unprepared for what they were witnessing. But Jesus had come to help, not to cause further problems to the toiling Apostles, and he immediately calmed them by saying, "Be of good cheer; it is I; be not afraid." The Apostles must have recognized him immediately, for no further concern on their part is recorded.

He next taught the Apostles the lesson of the miracle. Once again, as in so many examples, it was Peter who desired to experiment with the words and deeds of the Savior. "Lord, if it be thou," he declared, "bid me come unto thee on the water."

In the stilling of the tempest, Jesus had rebuked the Apostles because of their lack of confidence or their feelings of fear. Now Peter desired to overcome both. Jesus' response supported this desire. "Come," he said. He encouraged Peter to walk on the water with him.

The scene must have been electric with excitement. One can almost envision Peter as he cautiously slid over the side of the ship and started toward the Savior. "He walked on the water, to go to Jesus." But the wind became "boisterous." Although Peter had almost reached the Lord, the wind stirring the water made him afraid. It was then that he lost confidence in his ability to walk on the water. He began to sink and cried out, "Lord, save me." Jesus immediately stretched forth his hand and caught him. Then followed Jesus' teaching and mild rebuke: "O thou of little faith, wherefore didst thou doubt?" The rebuke was only for instructive purposes. In trying, even though he failed, Peter had in part succeeded. He now knew through his own experience that the power he witnessed in the Savior could be exercised by others in appropriate circumstances.[8]

A distinctive teaching on faith can also be gleaned from this miracle. Peter's attempt to walk on water was successful; only when his faith waned did his ability to exercise the power fail. Had Jesus forbidden Peter to walk on the water, it would have greatly diminished his confidence. The experience clearly demonstrated to Peter that faith itself was a principle of power, and that through it even the laws and forces of nature could be controlled. Further, that the source of this power (faith) was Jesus the Messiah.[9]

As in the stilling of the tempest, the miracle of walking on the water can be applied to life's general circumstances. The boisterous wind and the restless sea equate with the temptations of a tempestuous and sinful world. Peter's fear of the struggle and danger of the contrary winds and restless sea overcame his ability, and he cried out for help. The same situation exists in life. Many struggles and dangers confront our effort to "come" to the Savior. Sometimes we delay our cry for help. Sometimes it seems to go unheeded. But the example is clear. Just as Peter's fears and doubts were about to overpower his faith, the Lord extended his hand in comforting assurance so that Peter might not sink.[10] The Apostles knew that they, too, could use and exercise the power of the Lord, and they recognized more fully that the Lord was the source of that power.

Jesus entered into the ship with Peter, and the wind ceased. John reports that "they willingly received him into the ship: and immediately the ship was at the land whither they went."[11]

This miracle taught the Apostles many things. They would never again look upon the Lord as a mortal man. He had taught them from the beginning that he was the master of all. He was the Son of God, the promised Messiah, and they now acknowledged him as such. Through Peter's experience they learned that if their will was in complete harmony with Christ's, they could do all the miracles that he did.

The Raising of the Daughter of Jairus

Mark 5:22—24, 35—43

22. And, behold, there cometh one of the rulers of the synagogue, Jairus by name; and when he saw him, he fell at his feet,

23. And besought him greatly, saying, My little daughter lieth at the point of death: I pray thee, come and lay thy hands on her, that she may be healed; and she shall live.

24. And Jesus went with him; and much people followed him, and thronged him.

35. While he yet spake, there came from the ruler of the synagogue's house certain which said, Thy

daughter is dead: why troublest thou the Master any further?

36. As soon as Jesus heard the word that was spoken, he saith unto the ruler of the synagogue, Be not afraid, only believe.

37. And he suffered no man to follow him, save Peter, and James, and John the brother of James.

38. And he cometh to the house of the ruler of the synagogue, and seeth the tumult, and them that wept and wailed greatly.

39. And when he was come in, he saith unto them, Why make ye this ado, and weep? the damsel is not dead, but sleepeth.

40. And they laughed him to scorn. But when he had put them all out, he taketh the father and the mother of the damsel, and them that were with him, and entereth in where the damsel was lying.

41. And he took the damsel by the hand, and said unto her, Talitha cumi; which is, being interpreted, Damsel, I say unto thee, arise.

42. And straightway the damsel arose, and walked; for she was of the age of twelve years. And they were astonished with a great astonishment.

43. And he charged them straitly that no man should know it; and commanded that something should be given her to eat.

Cross-references:

Matthew 9:18—19; 23—26   Luke 8:41—42; 49—56
JST Matthew 9:25

This is the second raising of the dead discussed in the Gospels. Luke records the raising of the widow's son (see Luke 7:11—17) prior to this miracle. The raising of the daughter of Jairus is recorded by all of the Synoptics and left unrecorded by John. There are some minor differences here between Matthew and the other two Gospel writers. Matthew, as usual, records the bare facts. His eye is focused on the parties, the circumstances, the miracle performed, and the Lord's part in it. To Matthew, detail seems to be of minor importance. His view is directed to the teaching and to the witness of the divinity of Christ. For instance, Matthew records the daughter as dead, but in the other two she is only "near" death when Jairus comes to Jesus. However, Mark and Luke both describe Jairus as a man who believes his daughter is so near death that she may die before he can return home. Perhaps to Matthew her condition did not matter as Jairus approached Jesus, for she was dead when Jesus arrived at the house. Other divergent details of the miracle are similarly insignificant and can be ignored.

With regard to the circumstances surrounding the miracle, Mark and Luke agree, but Matthew is completely different and cannot be reconciled with the other two. It should always be remembered that none of the writers attempted to record the Master's daily activities.[12] Therefore, the placement of the miracle may not directly reflect the surrounding circumstances in any of the Gospels and need not concern us.

This miracle, perhaps more than any other, emphasized the pure love of Christ. Through it the Apostles would learn of Christ's boundless love and endless patience in bringing souls to him. They would also gain a firsthand witness of his power over death.

The teachings of the miracle are here reviewed topically.

Jesus and the rulers of the Jews. Jairus was a ruler in the synagogue at Capernaum. He may[13] or may not[14] have been one of those who came to Jesus on behalf of the centurion (see chapter 9). Perhaps he had been present when Jesus cast out the evil spirit from one in his synagogue.[15] But whatever the reason, it is obvious that Jairus displayed faith in Christ's ability to help him, no matter how limited or fragile that faith was.

There is much deeper significance here, however. A cursory reading of the scriptures might leave the impression that none of the rulers accepted or believed in Jesus, with the possible exception of Nicodemus.[16] From this miracle, however, it would appear that several (and perhaps many) of the rulers believed in him, not necessarily as the Messiah but at least as one who had powers from God. By coming to Jesus, Jairus showed confidence in the fact that He could and would help him. He approached Jesus with a desperate appeal. His daughter was dying, and the pain and distress of her impending death overcame the pressure of his peers and quickened his faith. He went to Jesus for a specific reason: he wanted the Lord to heal his daughter.

The development of faith. A great teaching on faith is evidenced in this miracle. It comes in the way the Lord nurtured the faith of Jairus and assisted its growth. The Synoptics record that Jairus begged Jesus in all earnestness to come with him to heal his "little daughter." The Lord treated the request with great compassion. Immediately he went with him, thus comforting Jairus, for he might have thought that Jesus would not come.

As Jesus traveled to Jairus's sick daughter, another miracle took place. A woman with an issue of blood (see chapter 13) touched Jesus and delayed the procession. Jairus waited patiently as the Lord took the time to extend his healing power to the woman. This, too, would have increased his belief that Jesus would and could help him. But now the event that Jairus so feared occurred: he received notice that his daughter was dead.

Regardless of his prior belief in the Lord, this news could have destroyed that hope and belief. Even the messenger expressed his hopelessness. "Thy daughter is dead," the messenger reported. "Why troublest thou the Master any further?" Luke records it more definitively: "Thy daughter is dead; trouble not the Master."

Seemingly death had conquered. But Jesus would not have Jairus's faith so easily destroyed. "Be not afraid, only believe," he told Jairus. In Luke it was recorded, "Fear not: believe only, and she shall be made whole." Although death had momentarily taken away the initial reason for his mission to the Lord, Jairus was assured that his daughter would yet be whole. His faith thus renewed and strengthened, apparently he showed no impatience or ingratitude at the Lord's delay.

When they reached the home, funeral ceremonies were already under way. Jairus made no objections when Jesus put the mourners out and declared that the girl "sleepeth." There was no doubt that she was dead, but to the Master death held no power. Quiet now, the bedchamber contained only Jairus, his wife, the Master, Peter, James, and John. Jesus took the girl by the hand and commanded her to arise. From the world of spirits he called her back, and she responded.

Astonished and overjoyed, Jairus and his wife received their daughter back once more. Their faith had been nurtured and enlarged. Their petition had been granted. No further mention of

Jairus is made, and it is not known what he did thereafter—but can there be any doubt that he would have glorified God and worshipped Him who had granted such blessings to his house?

Concerning the miracle, Jesus instructed Jairus to "tell no man what was done." But how could this instruction be complied with? Few witnessed the raising, but many knew of the death. It would be impossible to tell no one. Perhaps Jesus gave this instruction because he did not want the parents to glory in the miracle. He had carefully cultivated and developed the faith exhibited by Jairus. He did not want him to boast of the miracle and spread it abroad. He wanted Jairus to make of it a hidden treasure (later referred to in parable form, see Matthew 13:44) that once found, all may acquire. In truth, broadcasting such a miracle at this time might also have hindered the Lord's mission, for his enemies were always watching.

This was a private miracle, intended for Jairus, his family, and Peter, James, and John. It had generated true faith and belief from that kernel of faith that had brought Jairus to Jesus in the first place.

Unbelief. When Jesus arrived at the house of Jairus, the minstrels and mourners had already commenced the obsequies. Jesus spoke to them, that they, too, might believe. The girl was not dead but merely "sleepeth," he said. The result was illuminating. "They laughed him to scorn, knowing that she was dead." Although minor differences exist in phrasing between the three Synoptics, all of the writers agree on this point: the people knew the girl was dead. They had awaited the moment, perhaps hoping that Jesus could be brought in time, but when death came they lost all hope in him. They mocked his words. How could Jesus believe differently; he had just arrived. She was dead! Their spirit of unbelief contrasted sharply with Jairus's belief. Jairus had been totally pliant in Jesus' hands, awaiting his will. But from the mourners the Lord received only scorn.

Jesus "put them all out." They were no longer needed. He would not let their disbelief infect the others. Their despair at the death of the young girl was nothing compared to what they would undoubtedly feel when they found out what marvelous thing they had missed because of their unbelief.

Life in himself. The comparisons between the raisings of the dead in the Old Testament and those that Jesus performed have already been discussed (see chapter 2) and need not be reviewed again. But the emphasis is again noted. Jesus raised the girl by the command of his voice. He did not go through the contortions of Elijah and Elisha. He was the Life, and death had no power over him. This astonished Jairus and his wife. They witnessed the sign of his divinity. He was the Son of God.

The effect on the Apostles. This was a special teaching time for the Apostles. All of them would have followed as Jesus went to the house of Jairus. They would have observed the compassion and gentleness with which he nourished the faith Jairus needed to receive such a blessing. But he chose only Peter, James, and John to witness the actual raising from the dead. In this instance they alone witnessed the power of the Lord unveiled. They had been privy to the miracle of the first draught of fish at the time of their call as Apostles, and they would be with Christ at his transfiguration and his final prayer to his Father. They, with several others, would witness the miracle of the final draught of fish. Through their testimony they would strengthen their brethren. That they related their experience was obvious, for John, the only eyewitness to write a Gospel, did not mention it. It was a special witness for the Apostles. Influenced by this and other miracles John would later write, "In him was life; and the life was the light of men" (John 1:4).

This miracle was a personal one for Jairus and his wife and brought them the opportunity for salvation. It also provided a teaching time for the Twelve, particularly Peter, James, and John, so that they might know that Jesus was the Christ, the Savior of the world, the long-awaited Messiah.

The Barren Fig Tree

Mark 11:12—14, 20—24

12. And on the morrow, when they were come from Bethany, he was hungry:

13. And seeing a fig tree afar off having leaves, he came, if haply he might find

any thing thereon: and when he came to it, he found nothing but leaves; for the time of figs was not yet.

14. And Jesus answered and said unto it, No man eat fruit of thee hereafter for ever. And his disciples heard it.

20. And in the morning, as they passed by, they saw the fig tree dried up from the roots.

21. And Peter calling to remembrance saith unto him, Master, behold, the fig tree which thou cursedst is withered away.

22. And Jesus answering saith unto them, Have faith in God.

23. For verily I say unto you, That whosoever shall say unto this mountain, Be thou removed, and be thou cast into the sea; and shall not doubt in his heart; but shall believe that those things which he saith shall come to pass; he shall have whatsoever he saith.

24. Therefore I say unto you, What things soever ye desire, when ye pray, believe that ye receive them, and ye shall have them.

Cross-references:

Matthew 21:18—22   JST Matthew 21:20

This miracle was the Lord's final, private witness of record to the Apostles prior to his resurrection. Until now, the recorded miracles of Jesus were to life and the joy of its rewards. Here it was to death, and the certainty of the judgment and eventual punishment for evil.

There are at least four major teachings involved in this miracle:

1. Jesus is the Christ, the promised Messiah
2. The true principle of judgment
3. Hypocrisy and Judaism
4. The power of faith

Again there are discrepancies between Matthew and Mark. The principal difference concerns the time it took for the fig tree to wither and die. Matthew records that the tree died immediately (or at least gives that impression). Mark records that a day intervened between the cursing and the death. Yet even in Matthew's account, the day could have intervened. Note that Matthew records, "And presently the fig tree withered away."

The Lord was staying in Bethany during the last week of his ministry, traveling each day into Jerusalem. The scripture reports that on his journey this particular morning he was hungry. He saw a fig tree some distance ahead in full leaf. At the proper harvest time this would not have been unusual. But it was not "the time of figs." However, this tree seemed to indicate that it was. The fruit of the fig tree appears prior to the leaves, and by the time the tree is in leaf, the fruit is edible.[17] Jesus approached the tree, seemingly anticipating the fruit that might satisfy his hunger, but the tree provided no food. It had shown forth the promise of much fruit, but had produced nothing.

He who could perceive men's thoughts knew that no fruit was on the tree. But one of the great lessons of the miracle was to be learned through the anticipation he expressed as he and the Apostles approached the tree.

Jesus was the master teacher. He had drawn moral teachings from every facet of life for three years. He would now use this tree and the anticipation it caused to emphasize a parabolic teaching experience that the Apostles would never forget.

Jesus cursed the tree, commanding that "no man eat fruit of thee hereafter for ever." This was no angry response arising from personal disappointment. It was a teaching experience, vividly illustrating to the Apostles the consequences of rejecting him, his teachings, and his kingdom. The next morning Peter remembered the curse and drew Jesus' attention to the withered and dead tree. Now the teaching sequence began.

Jesus is the Christ, the promised Messiah. There were few more effective ways to show the power Jesus held over life and death than in this example. The Apostles had been with the Lord for three years. They had witnessed almost overwhelming human sorrows relieved by his great compassion. His patience and love had restored health, corrected disabilities and deformities, and raised the dead. Now they vividly saw before them the power of his wrath and judgment, and from this example of his control over life they would know that he gave his life voluntarily; no one could have taken it from him.

He taught the true principle of judgment. Jesus taught openly to the Pharisees that the Father had given him all rights to judgment (see John 5:22). He had undoubtedly instructed the

Apostles in private on the use and meaning of this power. The fig tree had promised fruit, according to its representation. When the time to harvest arrived, no fruit was available. The Lord cursed the tree in judgment of its hypocrisy and failure, and it received its just reward. The analogy was clear. The Lord held power over all things and would execute judgment on "they that have done good, unto the resurrection of life; and they that have done evil, unto the resurrection of damnation" (John 5:29).

Hypocrisy and Judaism of his day. The tree was a true hypocrite. It professed something it did not have. But it was cursed not because it did not have figs, but because it had falsely represented that it had them. This was Judaism's condition at the time of Christ.[18] The fig tree, as the emblem of Israel, was used many times by the rabbis in their teachings. The Jews had all of the vestures of professed religion, but they, like the tree, brought forth no fruit. The sin of Judaism was not that they were part of the chosen people and not that they had been given the only true religion; but that they had allowed it to degenerate into artificial religionism. They cried loudly to the world of the truth, yet they were mere pretenders themselves. With exactness they rigorously lived the outward law, and inwardly rejected him who gave it. The tree displayed the letter of the law with its full leaves but fruitless branches. Its destruction was a representation to Israel of their ultimate judgment if they persisted in their present course. But the time for final judgment upon Judah was not yet. Because they rejected the Messiah, the kingdom would be taken from them for a time, yet before the end another effort would be made to save them (see 2 Nephi 25:15—18).

Paul, using this analogy, defined the principle to the Romans. The Jews had boasted to others of their favored condition but had failed to learn themselves. They had declared themselves righteous because of the Law, healed and secure through its ritualistic observance. Believing themselves to be whole and at one with God, they rejected their Messiah (see Romans 2:17—27; 10:3—4). Upon their rejecting him, they were left barren, only the leaves of their professed belief hiding the nakedness of their pretentious show.

The power of faith. Jesus now taught the Apostles directly of faith and authority. Once again Peter expressed his recognition of the power Jesus had exercised. "Master, behold, the fig tree which thou cursedst." The Lord's answer led Peter away from the apparent vengefulness of the miracle.

"Have faith in God," Jesus answered. The Apostles could command mountains to move and they would go, but they must believe. "What things soever ye desire, when ye pray, believe that ye receive them, and ye shall have them." He cautioned them not to doubt, but to believe with all their hearts and pray earnestly. They, too, held the authority over nature, life, and death. The key to its use was faith. With it they could do all that Christ had done.

Through this personal miracle the Apostles could see that Jesus was the Lord of all. He could bless and save or curse and destroy. They might well adapt the symbolism of the tree not only to Judaism but also to themselves. The mercy and hope Jesus taught them must rule their use of his authority and power.

Their ministry was yet before them. In him, their Messiah, they saw the perfect example of what they must become.

Summary

The miracles discussed in this chapter were miracles of power, exposing the Apostles to Jesus' authority as the Son of God. He showed them he was Lord over all the earth. The elements and laws of nature were his to command and use for his purposes. He raised the dead and proved that death held no power over him. He cursed the fig tree and taught that he held power over life and death, both here and in eternity. All these evidences were given as a personal witness to the Apostles that he was the Son of God.

Through ordination, Christ gave his power and authority to the Apostles, and he instructed them in its use. They in turn could exercise this power only in faith, for undoubting faith in the Lord was the source of their authority.

A Gospel for All People

The Centurion's Servant

Luke 7:1—10

1. Now when he had ended all his sayings in the audience of the people, he entered into Capernaum.

2. And a certain centurion's servant, who was dear unto him, was sick, and ready to die.

3. And when he heard of Jesus, he sent unto him the elders of the Jews, beseeching him that he would come and heal his servant.

4. And when they came to Jesus, they besought him instantly, saying, That he was worthy for whom he should do this:

5. For he loveth our nation, and he hath built us a synagogue.

6. Then Jesus went with them. And when he was now not far from the house, the centurion sent friends to him, saying unto him, Lord, trouble not thyself: for I am not worthy that thou shouldest enter under my roof:

7. Wherefore neither thought I myself worthy to come unto thee: but say in a word, and my servant shall be healed.

8. For I also am a man

set under authority, having under me soldiers, and I say unto one, Go, and he goeth; and to another, Come, and he cometh; and to my servant, Do this, and he doeth it.

9. When Jesus heard these things, he marvelled at him, and turned him about,

and said unto the people that followed him, I say unto you, I have not found so great faith, no, not in Israel.

10. And they that were sent, returning to the house, found the servant whole that had been sick.

Cross-references:

Matthew 8:5—13   JST Matthew 8:9

This chapter deals with three miracles that gave evidence to the Twelve that the kingdom of God was not reserved for Israel alone. Their background and upbringing would have been traditionally Jewish. Thus anyone not "of the Covenant" was inferior. A Gentile could not be considered a fit candidate for the kingdom of God. In one of the early rabbinical lessons the Apostles might have studied, God was depicted as saying, "In the future world I shall spread for you Jews a great table, which the Gentiles will see and be ashamed."[1]

These three miracles served to overcome this doctrinal error. They have several things in common. First, they are public miracles. Second, the recipients of the miracles are Gentiles— heathens. And third, the miracles are granted as a reward for faith.

The healing of the centurion's servant is recorded by Matthew and Luke. Again there are differences. Historically it is viewed that Matthew primarily addressed himself to Jewish readers, whereas Luke wrote to the Gentiles. Matthew, writing principally to the Jews, emphasized the Lord's direct dealing with the centurion and commended his faith to them. Luke, on the other hand, writing principally to the Gentiles, emphasized the involvement of the local Jewish leadership in their praise of the Gentile to the Lord. Matthew persuades his countrymen that the Gentiles are favorable to the Church, while Luke invokes sympathy from the Gentiles in favor of the Jews.[2]

The events of the miracle took place in Capernaum, a Jewish community. A Roman garrison was stationed in the city, of whom the centurion, the commander of a hundred soldiers, was one. The scriptures do not indicate that the centurion had any previous contact with Jesus; however, that the centurion had heard of Jesus and had confidence in him is undeniable.

The "elders of the Jews" came to Jesus and presented the centurion's request. They praised the centurion and informed Jesus that he had been particularly good to them and was worthy of the request. The scripture specifically noted that the servant was "dear" to him. The centurion apparently loved Israel and had built their local synagogue. Jesus recognized the goodness of the man immediately, assented to their request, and left for the home of the centurion. Some must have gone ahead to tell the centurion that Jesus was coming, but the centurion did not feel worthy to have the Lord in his house. He sent other friends to intercept the Lord and indicate that the Savior's actual presence was not necessary for his request to be granted. He believed that the Lord had only to speak the word and his servant would be healed.

His message reflected his deep respect for and faith in Jesus. "Trouble not thyself," he stated through the messengers, "I am not worthy that thou shouldest enter under my roof." "Say in a word," his message continued, "and my servant shall be healed."

The centurion was a soldier, and used the example of his authority and command to illustrate his request. He believed that Jesus had the power to heal and expressed his great faith in him. He may not have received Jesus into his home, but he had certainly received Jesus into his heart. He had no doubt: "speak the word only," he said, "and my servant shall be healed."

This belief filled the Lord with admiration. His own chosen people had invited him into their houses, but had rejected him in their hearts. Yet this Gentile had recognized him as the king he was. Jesus "marvelled" at this centurion, and turning to the crowd that was following him he said, "I say unto you, I have not found so great faith, no, not in Israel." The miracle was granted and the servant healed.

Luke, writing primarily to the Gentiles, ended the miracle here. Matthew, however (writing to the Jews), extended the teaching, showing that the kingdom of God was for Jew and Gentile alike, and that the Jews would be in great jeopardy if they rejected the Gentiles.

According to Matthew, Jesus continued his teaching to those around him. He stated: "Many shall come from the east and west, and shall sit down with Abraham, and Isaac, and Jacob, in the kingdom of heaven. But the children of the kingdom shall be cast out into outer darkness." Jesus confirmed the great faith and hope of the centurion by declaring that the kingdom was not limited to members of the chosen race. This declaration would shake the very foundation upon which Judaism rested. It removed the very basis of their pride, intolerance, and self-righteous assurance. People from all the earth could enter the kingdom and be welcome. Israel's previous chosen condition was no longer an assurance that they would inherit the kingdom. The Lord was warning Israel that they were already in danger of forfeiting the promised blessings, for others were proving themselves more worthy than they.[3]

Later, Jesus would tell them, "The kingdom of God shall be taken from you, and given to a nation bringing forth the fruits thereof" (Matthew 21:43). If the Jews would not accept him, others would; indeed, they were anxiously awaiting the opportunity. The centurion was but the first fruits of a vast harvest outside the chosen people. The Jews' disbelief was a millstone about their necks. Their reliance on historical salvation would deny them the very blessings they longed for. John the Baptist had warned them of this early in his minstry: "Think not to say within yourselves, We have Abraham to our father: for I say unto you, that God is able of these stones to raise up children unto Abraham" (Matthew 3:9). But they had not learned. This plague of self-righteousness would continue until they crucified their Master, and beyond.

Paul and Barnabus later struggled with this concept. But they "waxed bold, and said, It was necessary that the word of God should first have been spoken to you [the Jews]: but seeing ye put it from you, and judge yourselves unworthy of everlasting life, lo, we turn to the Gentiles" (Acts 13:46). Paul, from Rome, again warned the Jews of their endangered position by saying, "Be it known therefore unto you, that the salvation of God is sent unto the Gentiles, and that they will hear it" (Acts 28:28).

Paul gave the Romans the analogy that perhaps best explains this teaching. He used a favorite comparison of the rabbis—the tame and wild olive tree. The tame tree was Israel, the chosen people; the wild branches, the Gentiles. Some of the tame branches would be broken off, he taught, and wild branches grafted in so that they might partake "of the root and fatness of the olive tree." The "root and fatness" was Israel, not in the day of Christ, but in the day that they were chosen. The branches were the tribes; the broken branches were the Jews and all those who would reject his teachings. The "wild" branches grafted in were the Gentiles. He declared that the branches were broken off because "of unbelief," and warned the Gentiles not to get high minded, "for if God spared not the natural branches, take heed lest he also spare not thee." Then he once again extended the promise to the Jews that if they would but give up their unbelief, God would graft them in again. In Paul's words:

> And if some of the branches be broken off, and thou, being a wild olive tree, wert grafted in among them, and with them partakest of the root and fatness of the olive tree;
>
> Boast not against the branches. But if thou boast, thou bearest not the root, but the root thee.
>
> Thou wilt say then, The branches were broken off, that I might be grafted in.
>
> Well; because of unbelief they were broken off, and thou standest by faith. Be not highminded, but fear:
>
> For if God spared not the natural branches, take heed lest he also spare not thee.
>
> Behold therefore the goodness and severity of God: on them which fell, severity; but toward thee, goodness, if thou continue in his goodness: otherwise thou also shalt be cut off.
>
> And they also, if they abide not still in unbelief, shall be grafted in: for God is able to graff them in again.
>
> For if thou wert cut out of the olive tree which is wild by nature, and wert graffed contrary to nature into a good olive tree: how much more shall these, which be the natural branches, be graffed into their own olive tree? (Romans 11:17—24.)

The kingdom was for all mankind.

The Daughter of the Syrophenician Woman

Matthew 15:22—28

22. And, behold, a woman of Canaan came out of the same coasts, and cried unto him, saying, Have mercy on me, O Lord, thou Son of David; my daughter is grievously vexed with a devil.

23. But he answered her not a word. And his disciples came and besought him, saying, Send her away; for she crieth after us.

24. But he answered and said, I am not sent but unto the lost sheep of the house of Israel.

25. Then came she and worshipped him, saying, Lord, help me.

26. But he answered and said, It is not meet to take the children's bread, and to cast it to dogs.

27. And she said, Truth, Lord: yet the dogs eat of the crumbs which fall from their masters' table.

28. Then Jesus answered and said unto her, O woman, great is thy faith: be it unto thee even as thou wilt. And her daughter was made whole from that very hour.

Mark 7:24—30

24. And from thence he arose, and went into the borders of Tyre and Sidon, and entered into an house, and would have no man know it: but he could not be hid.

25. For a certain woman, whose young daughter had an unclean spirit, heard of him, and came and fell at his feet:

26. The woman was a Greek, a Syrophenician by nation; and she besought him that he would cast forth the devil out of her daughter.

27. But Jesus said unto her, Let the children first be filled: for it is not meet to take the children's bread, and to cast it unto the dogs.

28. And she answered and said unto him, Yes, Lord: yet the dogs under the table eat of the children's crumbs.

29. And he said unto her, For this saying go thy way; the devil is gone out of thy daughter.

30. And when she was come to her house, she found the devil gone out, and her daughter laid upon the bed.

Cross-reference

JST Mark 7:22—23

Both Matthew and Mark record this miracle, and both texts are needed to draw the full meaning from it.

Upon occasion Jesus sought time alone with the Twelve. This trip to Phoenicia appears to have been one of those times, perhaps brought on by the recent execution of John the Baptist in Galilee or by the constant pressure from the people and his enemies. Apparently Jesus had previously performed miracles in Phoenicia (Mark 3:7—10), and his fame had preceded him.

This miracle itself has no distinguishing features. Its significance lies in the method of its performance and the teachings derived from it because of the nationality of the woman. Both writers emphasize that the woman was a heathen. She is called a Greek and a Syrophenician by Mark, and a Canaanite by Matthew. Jehovah of old had commanded Israel to "smite [the Canaanites] and utterly destroy them" (Deuteronomy 7:2). Now he would extend the blessings of the kingdom to them.

When the centurion's servant was healed, the concept that the gospel would go to both Jew and Gentile was demonstrated. Now it would be expanded. There were no interceding Jews, as was the case with the centurion. The miracle was performed on the borders of Judah, and no implications could be drawn except those that pertained to the relationship between the kingdom of God and the Gentiles. Thus the woman's race was clearly established. She was of a race cursed by God, hated and despised by the Jews. And yet the kingdom of God was offered to her.

Jesus "could not be hid" as he arrived in Phoenicia. This woman discovered his presence and went to him. She had a daughter possessed with a devil and wanted the Lord to cast it out. She addressed Jesus as, "O Lord, thou Son of David." Although a heathen, she was ready to accept Jesus as Israel's Messiah, but perhaps not yet as her Messiah. She obviously knew of Jesus, and even more she believed that he could and would heal her daughter.

She undoubtedly had heard of his claim to the Messiahship, yet perhaps to her he was but another god among her many gods, "for David had never reigned over her or her people."[4]

Her first plea to Jesus went unanswered, but she persisted. This was a teaching moment for the woman, that she would come to recognize who he was; and for the Apostles, that they might recognize for whom the kingdom had been established. Matthew records that the Twelve became impatient at the woman's persistence. They asked Jesus to "send her away; for she crieth after us." Possibly they were embarrassed, but more probably they still held fast to their old Jewish belief. They were the "chosen people," and he was their Messiah. They may still have considered the kingdom of God to be a Jewish kingdom.

But the woman would not be discouraged. Jesus finally responded to her and at first seemed to confirm the expressions of the Twelve. "I am not sent but unto the lost sheep of the house of Israel," he stated. But she would not be denied. She now had his attention and would not let the moment pass. She worshipped him and pleaded for his help. Jesus again discouraged her. "It is not meet to take the children's bread, and to cast it to dogs." Without malice or anger, she understood and accepted the relationship. The "children" were Israel, the chosen people; the "dogs" were the heathens. The children were within the kingdom, while she was yet without. But still she persisted.

Following the Lord in his analogy she continued, "Truth, Lord: yet the dogs eat of the crumbs which fall from their masters' table." Hers was a truly perceptive response. Her belief and hope in Christ had elevated her, not to a perfect knowledge, but to a true belief in him. Now she waited for his answer. The Apostles witnessing this experience observed that they had been shortsighted.

"O woman, great is thy faith," Jesus responded, and he granted the desired blessing. The Lord had initially delayed speaking to the woman that he might better teach her and the Twelve: first, that she would come to know with a surety Christ's identity and calling; and second, to dispel unacceptable Jewish traditionalism concerning the kingdom (which exhibited only prejudice and error).

The simple love of a Canaanite mother had triumphed. Not only Israel would be offered the kingdom. The Messiah was offering the rewards of the kingdom of God to Jew and Gentile alike.

The Feeding of the Four Thousand

Matthew 15:29—39

29. And Jesus departed from thence, and came nigh unto the sea of Galilee; and went up into a mountain, and sat down there.

30. And great multitudes came unto him, having with them those that were lame, blind, dumb, maimed, and many others, and cast them down at Jesus' feet; and he healed them:

31. Insomuch that the multitude wondered, when they saw the dumb to speak, the maimed to be whole, the lame to walk, and the blind to see: and they glorified the God of Israel.

32. Then Jesus called his disciples unto him, and said, I have compassion on the multitude, because they continue with me now three days, and have nothing to eat: and I will not send them away fasting, lest they faint in the way.

33. And his disciples say unto him, Whence should we have so much bread in the wilderness, as to fill so great a multitude?

34. And Jesus saith unto them, How many loaves have ye? And they said, Seven, and a few little fishes.

35. And he commanded the multitude to sit down on the ground.

36. And he took the seven loaves and the fishes, and gave thanks, and brake them, and gave to his disciples, and the disciples to the multitude.

37. And they did all eat, and were filled: and they took up of the broken meat that was left seven baskets full.

38. And they that did eat were four thousand men, besides women and children.

39. And he sent away the multitude, and took ship, and came into the coasts of Magdala.

Cross-reference:

Mark 8:1—9

This miracle is often compared to the feeding of the five thousand, but they do not merely duplicate each other. The uniqueness of each is emphasized by the following comparison:

Feeding of the Five Thousand	Feeding of the Four Thousand
• Five thousand men plus women and children fed	• Four thousand men plus women and children fed
• Time: extended afternoon and evening	• Time: three days
• Twelve baskets of food left over	• Seven baskets of food left over
• Audience: Jewish	• Audience: Gentile and heathen[5]
• Time of year: spring	• Time of year: late summer, early fall
• Single blessing performed on food[6]	• Two blessings performed on food

The substantial differences in this comparison emphasize the need for and purpose of the two similar miracles. Consider the following.

Circumstances. The feeding of the five thousand took place during an established event. Devout Jews were gathering to Jerusalem for the Passover, annually the most important religious event celebrated. As they traveled, they paused to hear Jesus, whom they recognized as an interesting teacher and a worker of miracles. The setting for the feeding of the four thousand was quite different. This multitude had come to Jesus not out of curiosity or religious zeal but as a result of his miracles, including the casting out of the evil spirit from the Syrophenician's daughter. He then performed a multitude of miracles (see chapter 1), healing the sick, lame, blind, dumb, maimed, and all manner of diseases. Included in this multitude of miracles was the healing of one deaf and dumb (see chapter 16). After Jesus had performed these miracles, the people "were beyond measure astonished, saying, He hath done all things well (Mark 7:37), and the multitude stayed with him.

Purpose. The feeding of the five thousand was given as a sign to the chosen people so that they might recognize in it the Old Testament expectation of the anticipated Messiah (see chapter 2). The multitude made this association, and tried to "take him by force, to make him a king" (John 6:15). In the feeding of the four thousand, there was no such reaction. The miracle served as a reward for faith, and further demonstrated to the Apostles that the gospel was universal and was not limited to the Jews alone. The Gentile multitude "wondered" and "glorified the God of Israel." Note that they glorified the "God of Israel." The Jews considered Jesus to be a teacher, but the heathen accepted him as a god (albeit they did not at first understand which god).

Jesus taught these people for three days. In that time he would have discussed many things concerning the kingdom of God and his divinity. The first fruits reaped through the centurion were now about to become a vast harvest. The Apostles witnessed firsthand what results could be obtained when the historical animosity harbored by the Jews was set aside.

An additional point of interest may be developed from the miracle. The Lord did not question the Twelve concerning the feeding of the four thousand as he had in the feeding of the five thousand. He merely stated that he would not have the multitude go away "fasting, lest they faint in the way."

The Apostles answered much as they had at the feeding of the five thousand, and said, "Whence should we have so much bread in the wilderness, as to fill so great a multitude?" Had they already forgotten the previous feeding? Had they not seen the many miracles so recently performed? Why did they respond in this manner? Several possibilities arise (even though their personal feelings are left unrecorded) that might explain their reaction. Seemingly, within these reasons lies the teaching of the miracle itself.

1. The Apostles had previously been taught the use of Christ's authority, but they had evidenced little control over it and seemed to lack confidence in the authority they held.

2. They may still have been hampered by the old traditional, Jewish belief. They were dealing with Gentiles. It was allowable to feed the Jews in the feeding of the five thousand, but were these Gentiles worthy of such a miracle?

3. They may have hesitated to call for the repetition of a previous miracle. They had witnessed requests for miracles from people that had had them granted, but they had also seen people condemned for asking. They may have hesitated out of fear (see Matthew 12:38–39).

4. They may have doubted whether Jesus would perform a duplicate feeding. The Apostles' reaction seemed to indicate this dilemma. As each new situation and difficulty arose, it appeared to be one that they could not solve themselves. They still had to learn to rely on the Lord.

Israel's history had been replete with miracles, but Israel had continually lacked reliance on the Lord. This was nowhere more vividly displayed than in their exodus from Egypt. They had been spared the death of the firstborn; they were led by miracles from Egypt through the Red Sea; they had been given manna; yet in all this they complained. As they journeyed, they ran out of fresh water and became thirsty. Again they chided Moses and murmured against him. (See Exodus 17:1–7.) They had learned nothing from the past. They were not confident in God's deliverance; they only demanded more.

The Jews of Christ's time had learned little from God's treatment of their ancient ancestors. In spite of all the miracles, past and present, the Jews still did not have faith in Jesus as the Messiah.

The Twelve had witnessed all or most of Christ's miracles. This witness would give them additional confidence and trust in the Lord and further develop their faith in him.

The Gentiles in this miracle had followed Jesus and thirsted after righteousness. He fed them living water and the bread of life, and confirmed their acceptance before him with this miracle. Again the Apostles witnessed that the Jews, although the chosen people, were not the only ones that would enter into the kingdom of God. Many would reject it, but none were to be excluded deliberately.

Summary

It is always somewhat presumptuous to classify miracles. There were probably greater miracles performed by Jesus than the three discussed in this chapter, but there were perhaps none more important to the future direction of the Church. These miracles evidenced that all were to be given the opportunity to be accepted into the kingdom of God. Peter would yet receive a vision that would lead him to Cornelius (see Acts 10), Paul would take the gospel to the gentile nations, and James would offer the positive solution before the Apostles and other Church leaders in Jerusalem when the propriety of enjoining Mosaic practices upon gentile converts was being considered (see Acts 15). However, in the miracles now under discussion the universality of the kingdom was witnessed to the Apostles, and it would remain with them so that later incidents could be decided correctly.

Jesus had been sent to the house of Israel first. That was the promise. But he had not been sent exclusively to the house of Israel, and that was the teaching. The kingdom of God was for all men—Gentile and Israelite, heathen and chosen. This instruction was preserved in these three miracles. Christ extended his compassion, mercy, and blessings to all. The Apostles needed this special instruction and witness so that they might be better prepared to serve Christ after his ascension.

Part Five

The Final Witnesses

They Ask of Him a Sign

The Raising of Lazarus

John 11:1—46

1. Now a certain man was sick, named Lazarus, of Bethany, the town of Mary and her sister Martha.

2. (It was that Mary which anointed the Lord with ointment, and wiped his feet with her hair, whose brother Lazarus was sick.)

3. Therefore his sisters sent unto him, saying, Lord, behold, he whom thou lovest is sick.

4. When Jesus heard that, he said, This sickness is not unto death, but for the glory of God, that the Son of God might be glorified thereby.

5. Now Jesus loved Martha, and her sister, and Lazarus.

6. When he had heard therefore that he was sick, he abode two days still in the same place where he was.

7. Then after that saith he to his disciples, Let us go into Judea again.

8. His disciples say unto him, Master, the Jews of late sought to stone thee; and goest thou thither again?

9. Jesus answered, Are there not twelve hours in the day? If any man walk in the day, he stumbleth not, because he seeth the light of this world.

10. But if a man walk in the night, he stumbleth, because there is no light in him.

11. These things said he: and after that he saith unto them, Our friend Lazarus sleepeth; but I go, that I may awake him out of sleep.

12. Then said his disciples, Lord, if he sleep, he shall do well.

13. Howbeit Jesus spake of his death: but they thought that he had spoken of taking of rest in sleep.

14. Then said Jesus unto them plainly, Lazarus is dead.

15. And I am glad for your sakes that I was not there, to the intent ye may believe; nevertheless let us go unto him.

16. Then said Thomas, which is called Didymus, unto his fellow-disciples, Let us also go, that we may die with him.

17. Then when Jesus came, he found that he had lain in the grave four days already.

18. Now Bethany was nigh unto Jerusalem, about fifteen furlongs off:

19. And many of the Jews came to Martha and Mary, to comfort them concerning their brother.

20. Then Martha, as soon as she heard that Jesus was coming, went and met him: but Mary sat still in the house.

21. Then said Martha unto Jesus, Lord, if thou hadst been here, my brother had not died.

22. But I know, that even now, whatsoever thou wilt ask of God, God will give it thee.

23. Jesus saith unto her, Thy brother shall rise again.

24. Martha saith unto him, I know that he shall rise again in the resurrection at the last day.

25. Jesus said unto her, I am the resurrection, and the life: he that believeth in me, though he were dead, yet shall he live:

26. And whosoever liveth and believeth in me shall never die. Believest thou this?

27. She saith unto him, Yea, Lord: I believe that thou art the Christ, the Son of God, which should come into the world.

28. And when she had so said, she went her way, and called Mary her sister secretly, saying, The Master is come, and calleth for thee.

29. As soon as she heard that, she arose quickly, and came unto him.

30. Now Jesus was not yet come into the town, but was in that place where Martha met him.

31. The Jews then which were with her in the house, and comforted her, when they saw Mary, that she rose up hastily and went out, followed her, saying, She goeth unto the grave to weep there.

32. Then when Mary was come where Jesus was, and saw him, she fell down at his feet, saying unto him, Lord, if thou hadst been here, my brother had not died.

33. When Jesus therefore saw her weeping, and the Jews also weeping which came with her, he groaned in the spirit, and was troubled,

34. And said, Where have ye laid him? They said unto him, Lord, come and see.

35. Jesus wept.

36. Then said the Jews, Behold how he loved him!

37. And some of them said, Could not this man, which opened the eyes of the blind, have caused that even this man should not have died?

38. Jesus therefore again groaning in himself cometh to the grave. It was a cave, and a stone lay upon it.

39. Jesus said, Take ye away the stone. Martha, the sister of him that was dead, saith unto him, Lord, by this time he stinketh: for he hath been dead four days.

40. Jesus saith unto her, Said I not unto thee, that, if thou wouldest believe, thou shouldest see the glory of God?

41. Then they took away the stone from the place where the dead was laid. And Jesus lifted up his eyes, and said, Father, I thank thee that thou hast heard me.

42. And I knew that thou hearest me always: but because of the people which stand by I said it, that they may believe that thou hast sent me.

43. And when he thus had spoken, he cried with a loud voice, Lazarus, come forth.

44. And he that was dead came forth, bound hand and foot with grave-clothes: and his face was bound about with a napkin. Jesus saith unto them, Loose him, and let him go.

45. Then many of the Jews which came to Mary, and had seen the things

which Jesus did, believed on him.

46. But some of them went their ways to the Pharisees, and told them what things Jesus had done.

Cross-reference:

JST John 11:2, 16–17

The Parable of Lazarus and the Rich Man

Luke 16:19–31

19. There was a certain rich man, which was clothed in purple and fine linen, and fared sumptuously every day:

20. And there was a certain beggar named Lazarus, which was laid at his gate, full of sores,

21. And desiring to be fed with the crumbs which fell from the rich man's table: moreover the dogs came and licked his sores.

22. And it came to pass, that the beggar died, and was carried by the angels into Abraham's bosom: the rich man also died, and was buried;

23. And in hell he lift up his eyes, being in torments, and seeth Abraham afar off, and Lazarus in his bosom.

24. And he cried and said, Father Abraham, have mercy on me, and send Lazarus, that he may dip the tip of his finger in water, and cool my tongue; for I am tormented in this flame.

25. But Abraham said, Son, remember that thou in thy lifetime receivedst thy good things, and likewise Lazarus evil things: but now he is comforted, and thou art tormented.

26. And beside all this, between us and you there is a great gulf fixed: so that they which would pass from hence to you cannot; neither can they pass to us, that would come from thence.

27. Then he said, I pray thee therefore, father, that thou wouldest send him to my father's house:

28. For I have five brethren; that he may testify unto them, lest they also come into this place of torment.

29. Abraham saith unto him, They have Moses and the prophets; let them hear them.

30. And he said, Nay,

father Abraham: but if one
went unto them from the
dead, they will repent.
31. And he said unto
him, If they hear not Moses

and the prophets, neither
will they be persuaded,
though one rose from the
dead.

In spite of all the Lord's miracles and teachings, the majority of the Jews did not accept him as the Messiah. Rather, they attempted to discredit him, and accused him of performing his miracles by the power of the devil.

Yet the Jewish leadership recognized that Jesus claimed to be the Messiah. On four recorded occasions they sought a sign from him to verify that claim, but they desired a very specific sign (see Matthew 12:38–40; Mark 8:11; John 2:18; 6:30). They had misinterpreted the signs and teachings of the Second Coming for those of the first; and so they looked for the sign of the coming of the Son of Man (see chapters 1, 2).

The Jews' concern about the Messianic claim centered around three specific issues.

Their political situation. They had been in bondage for the better part of the previous four hundred years, and they believed that the coming Messiah would grant them their freedom. They envisioned that he would take them from bondage, destroy their enemies, rain down judgment and disaster upon the wicked, and punish with death and destruction those who had oppressed Israel. This intense desire to be free from bondage had been a driving force for generations.[1]

Christ, however, offered freedom not of the body but of the soul. The intent of his first coming was to establish his spiritual kingdom. This did not promise freedom from bondage but freedom from sin. The Jews wanted an earthly king, not a spiritual one. The reaction of the multitude in the feeding of the five thousand exemplifies this. They wanted to force him to become their political king (see chapter 2). Israel's leaders were no different than the common people in this matter. They accepted Christ's signs, but refused his person. They wanted his kingdom, but on the earth, not in heaven.

Their earthly positions. The scribes, the Pharisees, and the chief priests had developed into the religious ruling class of the people. They had done this to preserve the nation for the coming Messiah. But in so doing, they became so imbued with their own self-importance that they would not sacrifice their position to accept the Messiah. The development of the teachings and doctrines of the Rabbinical Law had, over the centuries, elevated these positions. They denounced the sinner, the publican, the heathen, and the Sabbath breaker. They extolled the teacher, the rabbi, the Law, and the Pharisee. Meanwhile, Jesus came and ate with sinners and publicans, mingled with heathens, offered the kingdom to all, and denounced the ruling class as hypocrites and "whited sepulchres" (Matthew 23:27). To accept him meant that they must serve instead of being served, must give rather than receive, and must proclaim rather than be proclaimed.[2]

The things of the world. Although the rich man was symbolic in the parable of Lazarus and the rich man, he actually existed in practice. The Lord taught that there was no relationship between worldly things and the kingdom of God. Worldly things were of no importance, and acquiring them bore no relationship to attaining salvation.

Thus, for the leaders of the Jews to accept Jesus as their Messiah meant rejection of all they had thought of as being important.[3] They refused to give up all, even to gain all. Rather than accept and believe, they asked for another sign.

These specific requests for Messianic verification brought comments from the Lord on their lack of belief unless they had a sign (see John 4:48). So great was their curiosity pertaining to signs that even during his trial, as he was brought before Herod, Herod did not have justice on his mind; rather Herod "hoped to have seen some miracle done by him" (Luke 23:8).

However, the sign of the coming of the Son of Man was not to be theirs. The Master would answer their desires and give them a sign—not at their request and not the one they wanted, but a sign. The sign would be public and irrefutable, accompanied with doctrinal teachings that would leave them without excuse. This sign was encased within a parable and a miracle: the parable of Lazarus and the rich man, and the miracle of the raising of Lazarus.

The parable of Lazarus and the rich man compared two men. One was rich, clothed in purple (to indicate his noble heritage) and "fared sumptuously every day." He had all the things the world treasured. The other man was a poor beggar. He desired to eat leftovers from the rich man's table and was full of sores. His deplorable condition was accentuated by the "dogs [that] came and licked his sores."

Eventually the two men died. The rich man awoke in hell and was tormented. Looking up, he saw the beggar in Abraham's bosom, or paradise. The rich man cried to Abraham and asked that he might send down the beggar to dip "the tip of his finger in water" to cool the rich man's tongue, for he was "tormented in this flame." Abraham told the rich man that during his lifetime he had had his good things and the poor beggar had had evil things. But now the beggar was comforted and the rich man tormented. Furthermore, he said that a great gulf existed between them so that passage from one side to the other was not possible.

The rich man, now resigned to his fate, pleaded one more cause. He had five brothers yet alive upon the earth. He cried to Abraham to send the poor beggar down to testify to his brothers of their awful course. They apparently were living the same, senseless, error-filled life of the rich man. Abraham reminded him, "They have Moses and the prophets; let them hear them."

"Nay, father Abraham," the rich man replied, "but if one went unto them from the dead, they will repent."

But Abraham wisely responded, "If they hear not Moses and the prophets, neither will they be persuaded, though one rose from the dead." The rich man of the parable went unnamed; however, the poor beggar's name was Lazarus.

The rich man was symbolic of the Jewish nation at the time, particularly of the rulers. They had the "true treasure," and the rich man had all the good things of life that they revered. Poor Lazarus, the beggar, represented the impoverished, the sinners, heathens, publicans, and all that were despised by the Jewish leaders.[4] The reversed position in the spirit world exemplified that the things of the world had nothing to do with attaining the kingdom.

This example is reminiscent of the Twelve's response after a certain young rich man had left Jesus (he being unwilling to sell all that he had and give it to the poor so that he could follow Jesus; see Matthew 19:16–26). On that occasion the Lord said that it would be difficult for the rich to get to heaven—so difficult, in fact, that he compared it to a camel going through the eye of a needle. The Twelve's response was most interesting. Matthew reported that the "disciples . . . were exceedingly amazed, saying, Who then can be saved?" (Matthew 19:25). At that time they, too, perhaps felt that worldly success was related to heavenly attainment. But it was not so.

The great gulf between Lazarus and the rich man was a separation that existed at the time of the parable between paradise (the place where righteous and obedient spirits went after death to await the resurrection) and the spirit prison (where the disobedient went to await, perchance, some grace from God that would relieve them of their suffering). Jesus later bridged that gulf as he resided momentarily in the spirit world after his death and before his resurrection and there set in motion the missionary program. That program would take the gospel to those in the spirit prison.[5]

These seem to be the basic, doctrinal teachings of the parable of Lazarus and the rich man (summarily reviewed). In the parable, Abraham had testified that those still upon the earth had Moses and the prophets and could learn from them of the kingdom of God and the Messiah. But the rich man in the parable had wanted more; he had wanted a sign. The Pharisees, scribes, chief priests, and the people had the same resources that the rich man had—Moses and the prophets. But they also wanted a sign. The rich man wanted one sent from the dead to warn his five brothers; the Pharisees wanted a sign from Christ to satisfy their doubts. But Abraham said, "If they hear not Moses and the prophets, neither will they be persuaded, though one rose from the dead." Jesus had taught them the parable; next he gave to this "wicked and adulterous generation" the sign.

John is the only Gospel writer that reports the miracle of the raising of Lazarus. There is no explanation as to why the others did not, for they obviously would have known of it. On the subject of the house in Bethany the Synoptics say very little. Perhaps it had something to do with the raising, or perhaps they were afraid of bringing persecution upon Mary, Martha, and Lazarus, for they were known disciples of Jesus. Regardless of the reason, John preserved this spectacular miracle and the reaction of the Jews in splendid detail. That it was a deliberate, public sign is evident from the miracle itself.

Mary and Martha were sisters who lived in Bethany. They were very close to Jesus and aided him upon many occasions.[6] Lazarus, their brother, was stricken with an undisclosed illness, an illness serious enough that the two sisters sent messengers to Jesus. They did not request his return (perhaps because they knew that he could heal Lazarus by merely speaking the word). They did not even ask for a healing, but within their message their desire is seen. "Lord, behold, he whom thou lovest is sick." They knew that the Lord would know their desires, and he did.

Upon hearing the message Jesus said, "This sickness is not unto death, but for the glory of God, that the Son of God might be glorified thereby." This was to be a very special miracle. He declared its purpose before it occurred. He knew that Lazarus would die, and that he would raise him from the dead. The miracle would be for the glory of God and a sign of Jesus' divinity.

John records that Jesus loved Martha, Mary, and Lazarus, a statement probably inserted because of Jesus' delay, for it would become obvious after the miracle that he had allowed Lazarus to die, causing Mary and Martha to suffer the anguish of his death. But there was an exalted purpose to the miracle, and the suffering that took place was soon lost in the experience that Mary and Martha shared with their Lord.

Jesus remained two days longer in the same place, then announced his intention to return to Judea. His disciples became concerned, for they were in mortal danger there. Jesus responded with an analogy. "Are there not twelve hours in the day?" he said. "If any man walk in the day, he stumbleth not, . . . but if a man walk in the night, he stumbleth." A simple analogy. Jesus was the light of the world. Those who did not stumble followed him and his light. Those who were against him and disbelieved were in darkness and could not see, even at high noon, and would stumble and fall. Those who walked in the light need not worry that they might stumble, for as long as his mission was yet unfulfilled, he would not die.

Jesus then reminded the Apostles of Lazarus, but stated that he "sleepeth." He continued that they must go and awaken him

"out of sleep." The Apostles misunderstood and replied that if
Lazarus was sleeping, "he shall do well," thinking that if he was
sleeping, it was good for him and would aid in his recovery. But
Jesus did not allow misinterpretation or misunderstanding of this
miracle at any stage. "Lazarus is dead," he told them. Then he
again clearly stated the purpose of the miracle. "I am glad for
your sakes that I was not there, to the intent ye may believe."
Had he been there, or if he had but spoken the word, Lazarus
would have been healed; but the spectacular witness would not
have been made and the sign and teaching would have been left
incomplete.

Once his resolve to go was plain to the disciples, they went
with him. Thomas, often remembered for doubting at the Lord's
resurrection, displayed now a positive quality we prefer to remember him by as he boldly stepped forward and declared his
loyalty and love for the Savior: "Let us also go, that we may die
with him."

It took two days to return to Bethany. When they arrived,
Lazarus had "lain in the grave four days already." John notes that
many Jews had come to Bethany to comfort Mary and Martha.
Bethany was near Jerusalem, and the family was well known.
Their popularity may even have been enhanced by their association with Jesus. Fellow disciples would have given the family
comfort. Disbelievers and enemies may have been there in anticipation that Jesus would come, so that they might have cause to
again accuse him. Still others may have just been acquaintances,
for one of the most binding of the Jewish directives was "to obey
the Rabbinical direction of accompanying the dead, so as to show
honor to the departed and kindness to the survivors."[7] It was to
these people that Jesus came: to Mary and Martha, grieved at the
loss of their brother, and to the others—some friendly, some
indifferent, and some hostile.

When Martha heard that the Lord was approaching she left to
meet him, leaving Mary in the house. When she met Jesus she
expressed her innermost feelings: "Lord, if thou hadst been here,
my brother had not died." Her testimony was strong; she knew
that had Christ been there, he could and would have healed her
brother. Whether she knew that Jesus had deliberately delayed
his return or not is not indicated, but she knew that Lazarus was

dead and she sorrowed; yet her faith in the Lord was not diminished. "But I know, that even now, whatsoever thou wilt ask of God, God will give it thee," she continued. Did she dare to dream of divine interposition, but because of timidity was restrained from asking for such a blessing? She knew that Jesus had raised the dead, but was it her place to request such a miracle?

Jesus responded, "Thy brother shall rise again."

Martha willingly responded, for she had been taught the principle of resurrection. "I know that he shall rise again in the resurrection at the last day," she stated.

By her response Jesus knew that additional teaching was necessary. He stated forcefully, "I am the resurrection, and the life." He was the power that determined life and death. He would soon suffer death, but in so doing would also conquer it. But now, in advance of that day, he would witness and make clear his divinity. "Whosoever liveth and believeth in me shall never die." Continuing, he asked Martha, "Believest thou this?" She did believe, and she confessed her testimony of him as the Savior, the Son of God. She then went quickly and told Mary "the Master is come." Mary left immediately to go to Jesus, who was still outside the town.

As Mary left to greet Jesus, the Jews thought she was going to the tomb to mourn, and they followed her. But she led them to Jesus, and the public teaching and witness of his divinity began. Mary fell at Jesus' feet and, independent of Martha, repeated the same words of love and confidence to Jesus. The Lord observed these mourning people, truly humbled in the sorrow of death. John recorded that he "groaned in the spirit, and was troubled." No doubt he was affected by the worldly sorrow displayed at the physical death of Lazarus, but this was the Lord; he that took on himself all sorrows. Isaiah had declared centuries before that the Messiah would be "a man of sorrows, and acquainted with grief. . . . Surely he hath borne our griefs, and carried our sorrows." (Isaiah 53:3—4.) The grief of those who knew Lazarus was not false, and so it was that Jesus "groaned in the spirit," for he took upon himself their sorrow and suffering. He was also troubled that even those who believed in him did not fully understand. Jesus wept, and asked where they had laid Lazarus. His emotion caused mixed feelings among the crowd; some assumed that it was due to his grief for Lazarus, and noted "how he loved him." Others, even on this occasion, questioned why he had allowed such a friend to die. Under this criticism Jesus again groaned. He wept not only for the genuine sorrow of his friends, but for the disbelief and mockery of his enemies.

Christ arrived at the tomb, a cave with a large stone sealing its entrance, and asked that the stone be removed. Martha's response was practical. "Lord, by this time he stinketh: for he hath been dead four days." She knew when he had died. They buried the dead immediately in the hot climate of Judea, for without modern preservation techniques the decaying process began very rapidly. She still did not understand, and Jesus remonstrated her. "Said I not unto thee, that if thou wouldest believe, thou shouldest see the glory of God?"

They then took away the stone, and Jesus lifted up his eyes and said, "Father, I thank thee that thou hast heard me. And I knew that thou hearest me always: but because of the people which stand by I said it, that they may believe that thou hast sent me." He did not pray to receive authority or power, for he already possessed it.

The crowd must have been astonished at the opening of the tomb. Christ had twice before openly declared the purpose of this miracle, and now, before the entire crowd (friends and enemies alike), he openly declared it again. They had asked for a sign many times, and he had refused them on each of those occasions. Now he would give them a sign that they could not forget, and he would tell them plainly of its source. "Lazarus, come forth," he cried with a loud voice, so that all might hear. With the napkin tied around his face, and bound hand and foot with grave clothes, Lazarus came forth!

Christ is the life; in him is power over death; he is the resurrection. The Jews demanded a sign, and they received it. How could they doubt? John reports that many of the Jews who were there "believed on him," and no wonder. But others "went their ways to the Pharisees, and told them what things Jesus had done." Regardless of their intentions in doing this, the results were evil.

The Pharisees and chief priests gathered a council. The Sanhedrin existed at the time of Christ, but not in the original form. Since Herod had effectively broken it of its real power,[8] its activity was principally confined to ecclesiastical or semi-ecclesiastical causes,[9] and it was definitely shorn of the power to pronounce capital sentences.[10] The chief priest's office was still recognized by Rome, and councils were called to discuss local policy and religious matters.[11] But this council was different. This was, in all probability, the "standing 'council of the temple,' " whose members were also called "the elders of the priests." It consisted of fourteen members, and was a judiciary body. Although it did not ordinarily "busy itself with criminal questions, [it] apparently took a leading part in the condemnation of Jesus."[12]

"What do we?" they questioned themselves. "If we let him thus alone, all men will believe on him." Then they uttered their real concern: "The Romans shall come and take away both our place and nation." They were not concerned whether Jesus was the Messiah. They were like the rich man of the parable: concerned only with the things of the world, their political existence as a nation, and their prominence among the people. Caiaphas stepped forward and unwittingly acknowledged the Messiah's mission: "It is expedient for us, that one man should die for the people, and that the whole nation perish not." In his record John recognized that Caiaphas was prophesying the Savior's death. He would indeed die for all, but not to save the nation; rather he would save the souls of all who would follow him and live his commandments. No longer was it "if" they would kill him, but when and how: "Then from that day forth they took counsel together for to put him to death."

The miracle was over. It was the ultimate sign—the greatest teaching! The Jews understood both the miracle and the parable. John recorded that after the miracle many of the Jews "consulted that they might put Lazarus also to death (John 12:10). The Jews would not accept the teachings of Moses or the prophets. They made mockery of the Law, and as prophesied in the parable, they did not believe, "though one rose from the dead."

Jesus had given the Jews an indisputable sign. There could be no more doubt. Even in their council as they planned to kill him they acknowledged it: "What do we? for this man doeth many miracles." They sought to preserve a nation, but rejected the very man that could ensure its continuance and deliverance. They had asked of him a sign, and he had given it to them, yet "they took counsel together for to put him to death."

Malchus's Ear

Luke 22:49—51

49. When they which were about him saw what would follow, they said unto him, Lord, shall we smite with the sword?

50. And one of them smote the servant of the high priest, and cut off his right ear.

51. And Jesus answered and said, Suffer ye thus far. And he touched his ear, and healed him.

Matthew 26:51

And, behold, one of them which were with Jesus stretched out his hand, and drew his sword, and struck a servant of the high priest's, and smote off his ear.

Mark 14:47

And one of them that stood by drew a sword, and smote a servant of the high priest, and cut off his ear.

John 18:10

Then Simon Peter having a sword drew it, and smote the high priest's servant, and cut off his right ear. The servant's name was Malchus.

All four Gospel writers record the circumstances that gave rise to this remarkable miracle. Only Luke records the miracle itself, and John names the participants: the Apostle Peter and Malchus, the servant of the high priest. The setting to this event is most significant. It was the final day of Jesus' life. He had prophesied of Jerusalem's coming destruction, of problems in the latter days, and of his second coming. He held the last supper and instituted the sacrament. He saw his betrayer dip the sop and leave with malicious intent. He took the eleven and went to Gethsemane to atone for the sins of mankind. He asked Peter, James, and John to watch and pray as he prayed to his Father, and he returned to find them asleep. His personal anguish of the Garden completed, he said to his sleeping disciples, "Sleep on now, and take your rest: behold, the hour is at hand, and the Son of man is betrayed into the hands of sinners" (Matthew 26:45).

Jesus was in Gethsemane, across the brook Cedron, and his betrayal was near. John records that "a band of men and officers from the chief priests and Pharisees, cometh thither with lanterns and torches and weapons" (John 18:3). Luke describes the group as "a multitude." The rulers of Israel had dispatched the group with Judas at its head. Judas had agreed that for thirty pieces of silver he would take them to where Jesus was and point him out. Judas "knew the place" where Jesus would be (John 18:2); and so it was that he who would betray the Son of Man led them to him.

As the group approached, Jesus asked, "Whom seek ye?" (John 18:4). They responded, "Jesus of Nazareth," whereupon the Lord answered, "I am he." The group "went backward" in fear of him. Again they asked the same question and the Lord gave the same answer and requested that the Apostles be allowed to "go their way." (John 18:5–8.) Luke adds that when the arresting group approached the Lord, Judas "went before them, and drew near unto Jesus to kiss him." Jesus spoke directly to Judas and asked, "Betrayest thou the Son of man with a kiss?" (Luke 22:47–48.) Matthew reports that Judas actually kissed the

Savior; that it was the "sign" that Judas had prearranged to identify the Lord to the arresting officers (see Matthew 26:48). Mark
agrees with Matthew concerning the sign of the betrayal and with
Luke about the multitude. He also attests to the fact that the
arresting officials had swords and staves. (See Mark 14:43.)

In this instance the differences between the Gospels add to
what otherwise would have been a very sketchy report. By
combining them, the scene can be summarized as follows:

1. The arresting group was large, but certainly not a "multitude" in the sense used to describe situations such as the feeding
of the five thousand.

2. Judas was at their head.

3. A kiss had been predetermined as the sign agreed upon to
single out the Lord for arrest. (A kiss was a common form of
salutation in that day.)

4. Some of the arresting group were armed with swords and
staves.

Thus the scene was set for Jesus' arrest.

As the scenario developed, Peter perceived an immediate
danger to the Lord's life. One of the Apostles asked the question,
"Lord, shall we smite with the sword?" Thereupon Peter drew his
sword, and with the love he had for the Savior and the natural
courage of his heart, struck Malchus, a servant of the high priest
and one of those that would take Jesus. The blow struck
Malchus, cutting off his right ear.

Jesus immediately calmed the situation: "Put up again thy
sword into his place: for all they that take the sword shall perish
with the sword" (Matthew 26:52). He reminded the Apostles of
his power. He need only call to his Father, and legions of angels
would be at his command; but that would defeat the purpose of
his life. Jesus then restored the ear as it was before.

This is the only healing of record where the wound was
caused by external violence. Jesus restrained the anger of the
Apostles with a mild rebuke. "Suffer ye thus far," he stated. They
had come this far with him, and they should not consider actions
that might destroy them, their past work, and work yet to be
performed. Through this act of compassion Jesus fulfilled and
exemplified his own teachings. "Love your enemies," he taught,
and "do good to them that hate you" (see Matthew 5:44).

No mention is made of any reaction by the arresting officials to either the blow or the healing. In plain view of all who had witnessed the blow, before those who would have heard the cries of pain and seen the blood, Jesus touched the injured ear and healed it. Still the officials pursued their goal.

The Apostles quickly scattered and fled in fear of their lives. According to Matthew's account, Judas, remorsefully aware of his part in this evil plot, killed himself (see Matthew 27:3–5). All that the Lord had taught his Apostles would be given to them again, but on this night they deserted him. In the future the Apostles would establish the Church in many nations and be responsible for the conversion of many souls. They would testify of Christ and give their lives for the work. But on this night of betrayal the Savior stood alone, and in one last miraculous act of mercy and compassion, witnessed to them all that he was the Messiah.

It Is I 12

Passing Unseen (After the Resurrection)

This chapter contains three more examples of the miracle of passing unseen, first discussed in chapter 4. These instances occurred after the Resurrection, while the previous examples were before the Resurrection. The previous uses of this miracle were to extricate Jesus from the pressure of an angry mob bent on killing him. These later miracles involve loved ones, friends, and disciples. These people knew Jesus personally, yet in each case they were unable to recognize him until he wanted them to do so. Two of the miracles are recorded in John, and the third in Luke with a cross-reference to Mark.

Jesus taught the disciples of his coming resurrection, yet it seemed difficult for them to understand. "After all that Christ had taught concerning his rising from the dead on that third day, the Apostles were unable to accept the actuality of the occurrence; to their minds the resurrection was some mysterious and remote event, not a present possibility."[1] Although Jesus had raised others from death, it was to a renewal of mortality. Now the disciples must comprehend his immortality. It appears that this miracle was used to enhance the disciples' understanding, that they might better testify of his resurrection.

Mary at the Tomb

John 20:14—17

14. And when she had thus said, she turned herself back, and saw Jesus standing, and knew not that it was Jesus.

15. Jesus saith unto her, Woman, why weepest thou? whom seekest thou? She, supposing him to be the gardener, saith unto him, Sir, if thou have borne him hence, tell me where thou hast laid him, and I will take him away.

16. Jesus saith unto her, Mary. She turned herself, and saith unto him, Rabboni; which is to say, Master.

17. Jesus saith unto her, Touch me not; for I am not yet ascended to my Father: but go to my brethren, and say unto them, I ascend unto my Father, and your Father; and to my God, and your God.

Cross-references:

Luke 24:1—10   JST Luke 24:14

After the crucifixion the body of Jesus was hastily taken down from the cross, quickly prepared for burial, and placed in the tomb. Some disciples had intended to reopen the grave after the Sabbath to further adorn the body of the Lord; yet even this act of love displayed their lack of understanding concerning the Resurrection. Had they fully understood his rising they would not have anticipated the need for further bodily adornment.

On the first day of the week, one of Christ's female disciples came to the sepulchre. Her name was Mary Magdalene. She was alone, according to John, but in Luke's version others were with her. They had brought spices to further adorn the Lord's body. When they arrived at the tomb, the stone covering its entrance had been rolled away. Two angels sitting at the entrance to the tomb spoke to the women, and asked why they sought the living among the dead. They further declared that Jesus had risen and that the women should return and tell the Apostles. Mary, now alone, pondered this announcement. She was weeping, and when the angels asked why, she responded, "Because they have taken away my Lord, and I know not where they have laid him" (John 20:13). She turned and saw the Lord, "and knew not that it was Jesus." They conversed briefly, but she still did not recognize him.

Jesus then addressed her personally and called her by name. It was then that she recognized him and responded, "Master." Apparently she moved toward him, perhaps to embrace him, but the Lord admonished her not to touch him and told her to go and tell the Apostles that he had risen.

On the Road to Emmaus

Luke 24:13—16, 31

13. And, behold, two of them went that same day to a village called Emmaus, which was from Jerusalem about threescore furlongs.

14. And they talked together of all these things which had happened.

15. And it came to pass, that, while they communed together and reasoned, Jesus himself drew near, and went with them.

16. But their eyes were holden that they should not know him.

31. And their eyes were opened, and they knew him; and he vanished out of their sight.

Cross-reference:

Mark 16:12—13

Two disciples were walking to Emmaus, "about threescore furlongs" from Jerusalem. They were discussing the monumental events concerning Jesus. They undoubtedly spoke of Christ's recent trial and crucifixion. They probably recounted the stories that surrounded the disappearance of Jesus' body, and pondered the testimony of those who had said they had seen him.

Jesus drew near and walked with them. He must have joined them in a normal manner, for nothing miraculous is recorded concerning this. "But their eyes were holden that they should not know him." Jesus talked to them, asked them questions about the subject of their conversation, and noted that they were sad. One of the two disciples was named Cleopas; the other remains unnamed, but is generally thought to be Luke.[2] Cleopas responded to the question and asked Jesus if he were "only a stranger in Jerusalem" (Luke 24:18). While continuing their journey, they rehearsed the events of the crucifixion to him, and in due time they arrived at Emmaus. They asked Jesus to stop and dine with them, still not recognizing him. Jesus agreed. He took bread, broke it, blessed it, and gave it to them. "And their eyes were opened, and they knew him; and he vanished out of their sight."

On the Shore of Galilee

John 21:4

4. But when the morning was now come, Jesus stood on the shore: but the disciples knew not that it was Jesus.

The last of these miracles was briefly mentioned earlier (see chapter 7) in connection with the miracle of the last draught of fish. Peter and six others had been waiting in Galilee for further instructions from the Lord. They had already seen him after his resurrection. They decided to go fishing, and spent the night casting their nets without success. As the morning drew near, they headed toward the shore. A figure was standing on the shore, "but the disciples knew not that it was Jesus." They conversed with him, and he then provided the miracle of the final draught of fish. At that point John recognized that it was the Lord and informed Peter. The group went ashore, ate of the meal that the Lord had prepared, and received his instructions.

The people involved in these miracles were all disciples of the Lord. Mary had been converted and forgiven of her sins. The Apostles were with him almost continuously for three years during his ministry. In the case of Cleopas and the unnamed disciple, their previous acquaintance with the Lord is not known, but from their discussion it is obvious that they had known him.

In these instances the Lord simply did not want his disciples to recognize him.

He apparently used this miracle for clarification and witness. No resurrection had occurred prior to that of Jesus Christ. Consequently, his disciples, including the Apostles, must clearly understand two things: first, that he had risen; and second, exactly what his resurrection meant. He had told them several times prior to his death that he would rise again, but they had not understood. When Mary and the women told the Apostles that Jesus had risen, their "words seemed to them as idle tales, and they believed them not" (Luke 24:11). Peter ran to the tomb and looked in. He saw the linen clothes by themselves; the body was gone. He departed, "wondering in himself at that which was come to pass." Clearly he did not fully comprehend. The Lord would use this miracle to bring to the memory of the Apostles and the disciples precious teachings and instructions that they had previously received. He did this to strengthen their witness of him.

Encouraged by the Lord's questions, the disciples on the road to Emmaus rehearsed the circumstances of their acquaintance with the man named Jesus. They asked him to dine, and then Jesus performed the ordinance of breaking and blessing the bread. With this they knew him. Their eyes were opened and the Spirit bore witness; their bosoms burned, and they received a testimony of the resurrected Christ.

The Apostles had gone to Galilee to await another appearance of the Lord. Rather than merely appear to them and give them instructions, Jesus duplicated the miracle that he had used when he first called the Apostles to follow him. John immediately recognized the circumstance; they all then recognized the Lord and received his teachings.

Mary's case is somewhat different. She was the first to see the resurrected Lord. She, too, had not fully understood the teachings concerning his coming forth. The Lord's questions invoked her innermost feelings concerning him. When he called her by name, the personal manner became familiar to her. She recognized him, even though she could not touch him. She could now testify that he had risen, and she was instructed to do so.

The miracle in each case allowed Jesus' Apostles and other disciples time to recall their former associations with him. In the future when they testified of his resurrection, they would be asked to explain how they knew it was so. Thanks to the Lord's use of this miracle, the experience was clear to them, and they would be able to testify with assurance that the Lord had been resurrected. Mary could say that she had seen him, but more important, that he addressed her as he always had—in the same manner, with the same tone, generating the same feelings.[3] The disciples on the road would remember their conversation with him and would report that he broke bread and blessed it as before.[4] The Apostles saw him several times, but after this miracle their testimony was even more secure.

The Lord declared his resurrection in many ways to his disciples. He talked with them, walked with them, allowed them to touch him, and permitted them to see him with their own eyes. On one of these occasions he declared that he was not a "spirit" as supposed, but that his resurrected body was "flesh and bones" (Luke 24:36—39). These physical, sensory experiences added strength to their witness. But the witness invoked by this miracle (to Mary, the disciples on the road, and the Apostles) was an emotional and spiritual witness of him, given so that the disciples might not just believe but know, and might witness that he was indeed the Christ.

Part Six

"That They May Believe That Thou Hast Sent Me"

The Source
of His Power

13

The Nobleman's Son

John 4:45—54

45. Then when he was come into Galilee, the Galileans received him, having seen all the things that he did at Jerusalem at the feast: for they also went unto the feast.

46. So Jesus came again into Cana of Galilee, where he made the water wine. And there was a certain nobleman, whose son was sick at Capernaum.

47. When he heard that Jesus was come out of Judea into Galilee, he went unto him, and besought him that he would come down, and heal his son: for he was at the point of death.

48. Then said Jesus unto him, Except ye see signs and wonders, ye will not believe.

49. The nobleman saith unto him, Sir, come down ere my child die.

50. Jesus saith unto him, Go thy way; thy son liveth. And the man believed the word that Jesus had spoken unto him, and he went his way.

51. And as he was now going down, his servants met him, and told him, saying, Thy son liveth.

52. Then inquired he of them the hour when he began to amend. And they said unto him, Yesterday at the seventh hour the fever left him.

53. So the father knew that it was at the same hour, in the which Jesus said unto him, Thy son liveth: and himself believed, and his whole house.

54. This is again the second miracle that Jesus did, when he was come out of Judea into Galilee.

Jesus repeatedly told the Jews that God was his Father, and that his Father had given him the authority to do God's work (see John 5, 6, 7, 8). He spake "as one having authority, and not as the scribes" (Matthew 7:29). The two miracles dealt with in this chapter emphasize this principle.

The healing of the nobleman's son is often compared to the healing of the centurion's servant, for the blessing was granted by the word of Christ while some distance from the afflicted person. The nuances of the miracle would seem to indicate that the nobleman was driven to Jesus by the anguish he felt at the anticipated loss of his son, and not by any inner conviction of Christ's divinity. Only John records the miracle.

Jesus had been to a feast in Jerusalem prior to coming to Cana of Galilee, and apparently had performed many miracles there. None are recorded, but we infer them from John's introduction to the miracle: "Then when he was come into Galilee, the Galileans received him, having seen all the things that he did at Jerusalem at the feast." This knowledge, coupled with the nobleman's pressing need, brought him to Jesus.

It has been speculated that the nobleman was one of the officers of the court of Herod Antipas.[1] Some specifically identify him as Chuza,[2] Herod's steward, based on Luke's statement that "Joanna the wife of Chuza Herod's steward . . . ministered unto him of [her] substance" (Luke 8:3).

The nobleman lived in Capernaum and his son was sick, "at the point of death." He came to Jesus and "besought" him to heal his son; but more than this, he requested that Jesus "come down" to his home to perform the healing. He seemed to believe that Jesus, as the great rabbis of Israel did, must be present to invoke the blessing upon his son, thereby adding his presence to the strength of his supplications to God. Jesus rebuked the nobleman's request, not because he asked for a miracle, but because of his lack of understanding. He responded: "Except ye see signs and wonders, ye will not believe." "Except ye see me come and lay my hands on the head of your son, as ye are aware I have done to others, ye will not believe that he shall be healed. Do ye not know that it is written of me 'He sent his word, and healed them?' "[3] The nobleman appeared to have faith in Christ as a miracle worker and healer but not as the Messiah.

The nobleman seemingly took no offense at Jesus' remark, for he persisted in his goal. He again requested Jesus to "come down" ere his son die. Jesus now taught the man, the Apostles, and others that were with him of his authority. The distance from the sick son meant nothing—in Jesus was the life. "Go thy way; thy son liveth," Jesus commanded.

With his faith strengthened by the promise of the Lord, the nobleman went his way. Capernaum was some twenty miles away. He could readily have reached his home that evening, for it was early afternoon when he spoke with Jesus, but for some reason he tarried. He spent the night either in Cana or between Cana and Capernaum, and in the morning continued the journey to his house. As he journeyed, he met his servants coming to tell him the news: his son lived! He asked them the "hour when he began to amend." They responded that the fever left him in the seventh hour on the previous day. The hours of the day were calculated from sunrise forward, so the boy would have been healed about 1:00 P.M. of the previous day.[4] The father must have noted the hour when he left Jesus, for John records that he "knew that it was at the same hour." This conversation perhaps betrayed the reservation remaining in the nobleman's mind, but knowing his son had been healed strengthened his faith again.

Jesus had performed two miracles on this occasion; the son's body was healed, and the father's spirit was enlightened. As the Psalmist had said, "He sent his word, and healed them, and delivered them from their destructions" (Psalm 107:20). All those involved in this miracle ultimately recognized the Savior's authority. The nobleman and all his house were converted, and the Apostles were strengthened.

To save the soul was more important than to heal the body. The physical healing, as with all of the miracles, was secondary to the spiritual growth. But to accept these blessings meant recognizing whence the blessing came. Such was the case with the nobleman and all his house.

The Woman with an Issue of Blood

Mark 5:25—34

25. And a certain woman, which had an issue of blood twelve years,

26. And had suffered many things of many physicians, and had spent all that she had, and was nothing bettered, but rather grew worse,

27. When she had heard of Jesus, came in the press behind, and touched his garment.

28. For she said, If I may touch but his clothes, I shall be whole.

29. And straightway the fountain of her blood was dried up; and she felt in her body that she was healed of that plague.

30. And Jesus, immediately knowing in himself that virtue had gone out of him, turned him about in the press, and said, Who touched my clothes?

31. And his disciples said unto him, Thou seest the multitude thronging thee, and sayest thou, Who touched me?

32. And he looked round about to see her that had done this thing.

33. But the woman fearing and trembling, knowing what was done in her, came and fell down before him, and told him all the truth.

34. And he said unto her, Daughter, thy faith hath made thee whole; go in peace, and be whole of thy plague.

Cross-references:

Matthew 9:20—22   Luke 8:43—48

This miracle teaches several doctrines, but none more pointedly than that pertaining to Christ's authority. It is recorded by all three Synoptics. Mark is used here as the primary text, but all the Synoptics agree on the miracle's main points and the circumstances surrounding it.

The circumstances of this healing are unique, for they are contained within the framework of yet another miracle. Jairus had come to Jesus to request the healing of his sick daughter, and Jesus had agreed to go with him to his house where the sick child lay. This miracle occurred while Jesus was on the way to Jairus's house. The woman had apparently overheard the discussion between Jairus and Jesus, and she joined the crowd that thronged about Jesus as he walked with Jairus toward his home.

The woman had an "issue of blood," an ailment involving frequent hemorrhaging. The ailment had been with her for twelve years. She had made many efforts to cure the disease. The scripture notes that she had "suffered many things of many physicians," for this was a disease which had several prescribed cures. One Talmud treatment for the ailment reads: "Take of the gum of Alexandria the weight of a zuzee (a fractional silver coin); of alum the same; of crocus the same. Let them be braised together, and given in wine to the woman that has an issue of blood. If this does not benefit, take of Persian onions three logs (pints); boil them in wine and give her to drink, and say, 'Arise from thy flux'."[5] Throughout the years she had undoubtedly used this and many other mystical remedies prescribed by the physicians of the day.

Edersheim states: "On one leaf of the Talmud not less than eleven different remedies are proposed, of which at most only six can possibly be regarded as astringents or tonics, while the rest are merely the outcome of superstition, to which resort is had in the absence of knowledge."[6] One of those superstitions required the carrying of "the ashes of an Ostrich-Egg, carried in summer in a linen, in winter in a cotton rag."[7] It is easy to see how, after trying such "remedies" for twelve long years, she had spent "all that she had, and was nothing bettered, but rather grew worse."

The woman, like Jairus, had heard of the healings that Jesus had performed and had come to him to be healed. But unlike Jairus, who openly sought Christ out, she had conceived in her heart that if she could but touch his clothes or the hem or "border of his garment" she would be made whole.

This hem or border was not the bottom of the skirtlike

garment traditionally worn at that time, but a special border applied to the upper shirt, or shawllike garment worn over the shoulders.[8] It was a mark of the Levitical Priesthood, commanded by God to be worn. "And the Lord spake unto Moses, saying, Speak unto the children of Israel, and bid them that they make them fringes in the borders of their garments throughout their generations, and that they put upon the fringe of the borders a ribband of blue: And it shall be unto you for a fringe, that ye may look upon it, and remember all the commandments of the Lord, and do them . . . and be holy unto your God" (Numbers 15:37—40; see also Deuteronomy 22:12). The Jews wore this shawl to indicate to the people that they were Pharisees or scribes and that they lived the commandments and were accounted teachers of the Law. But the symbolism of the shawl had deteriorated, and Jesus rebuked what had become a meaningless practice. "But all their works they do for to be seen of men: they make broad their phylacteries, and enlarge the borders of their garments" (Matthew 23:5). Some portions of the accustomed dress of the teachers of the time of Jesus was absolutely necessary to "publicly read or 'Targum' the scriptures, or exercise any function in the Synagogue."[9] It can therefore be assumed that Jesus wore these garments. However, "we may safely assume [that he would] go about in the ordinary, . . . not in the more ostentatious, dress, worn by the Jewish teachers of Galilee."[10]

The woman eventually succeeded in touching the Lord's garment, and immediately "she felt in her body that she was healed of that plague." Upon being healed, she attempted to shrink secretly back into the crowd.

Her faith in the Lord was great, but it was incomplete. She did not understand that her faith had drawn a tangible power from Jesus, and without it she would not have obtained the blessing. The power Christ possessed was from his Father and was not inherent in his garments or in the flesh and bone of his body. The healing power had not come from him against his will, even though it had been drawn from him by the woman's great faith. There was to be no misunderstanding as a result of this miracle; therefore, he did not allow the woman to escape unnoticed after she had been healed.

Jesus immediately knew "that virtue had gone out of him."[11] He turned, looked at the crowd, and asked, "Who touched my clothes?" The disciples were not aware of what had taken place. They, along with a large crowd, were anxiously following Jesus to the home of Jairus, eagerly anticipating the coming miracle involving Jairus's daughter.

Therefore, when the Lord asked who had touched him, the disciples responded incredulously. "Thou seest the multitude thronging thee, and sayest thou, Who touched me?" But Jesus had perceived that "virtue had gone out of him." His question was not directed to his disciples but to the woman.

The woman was being called before her Lord and Savior to account for her actions. Her intentions had been pure and her faith sure. Therefore, "fearing and trembling, knowing what was done in her, [she] came and fell down before him, and told him all the truth." With love and compassion the Lord responded, "Daughter, thy faith hath made thee whole; go in peace, and be whole of thy plague."

Christ would not withhold a blessing from this faithful woman, but he wanted to teach her, the Apostles, and the multitude that he was the source of the healing power, and that it was extended by his will. That the woman had drawn upon it by her faith was true, but the reservoir of the power and the well from which the life-giving water had been drawn was Jesus Christ. Faith had made her cure possible, but Christ had done the healing.

A Kingdom for All People

Sin and Leprosy

The Law of Moses and the Levitical ordinances created a very orderly society. This orderliness separated the Jews from their neighbor nations. But the ordinances were given for reasons other than merely creating this orderly society. They created a relationship—not just among themselves, but with God. The Law was to bring the chosen people closer to God and to direct every moment of their lives toward him.

Conversely, the Law was also evidence of their sinfulness; for through it, they came to know the cause of their separation from God. Yet it provided the means whereby they could symbolically cleanse themselves from sin and regain the purity God demanded. By complying with the Law they were schooled in the two great commandments. The first was to love God—living the Law resulted in spiritual growth and reminded them to do all things with God in mind. The second commandment was to love their neighbor, and regulation upon regulation dictated exactly how this was to be done. The Law was their schoolmaster through which they could again achieve a closeness with God that had been lost through sin.

To be cast out of this order or deprived of its regulations meant exclusion from God himself. The greatest symbol under their Law that exemplified this condition was the disease of leprosy.[1] The Talmud said, "These four are counted as dead, the blind, the leper, the poor, and the childless."[2] Even though sin was often accounted as the reason for blindness, poverty, and childlessness, individuals with these afflictions were nonetheless accepted within the community and society. But the leper was different. He was morally dead, cursed of God; his disease was a symbol of sin and uncleanliness.[3] The leper was excluded from the camp of Israel and considered to be a loathsome member of the living dead (see Leviticus 13:46; Numbers 5:2—4).

The consequence of sin was spiritual death, and God set leprosy aside as an example to Israel of that principle. It was the living definition of sin. It progressed slowly, eating the flesh, thriving and increasing, sustaining itself upon the body, with the inevitable conclusion—death.[4]

The results of sin were looked upon in like manner. To the Jews, God was a God of the living, not the dead. The leper was thus excluded from Jewish life in the same manner that the sinner was excluded from the presence of God.[5]

Only Israelite lepers were regulated among the chosen people. Strangers and sojourners in their land were expressly exempted from the ordinances and regulations of the Law regarding leprosy.[6] An Israelite had to cry "Unclean" as another approached, had to wear a torn garment, and had to cover his lower lip.[7] God could easily have made all sickness unclean, for illness often led to death. But he took one example, leprosy, and made it a visible sign of sin's nature. It was the sign that evil was not from nor acceptable to God and that those who were sinful could not dwell with him. It alone was selected as a witness against sin and its results.[8] "This did not mean that the disease borne by any individual attested that he was a worse sinner than his fellows, only that the disease itself was a symbol of the ills that will befall the ungodly and rebellious."[9]

The fact that leprosy was incurable added to the reasons why it was singled out. So closely connected was the disease with sin that a man's true repentance was recognized as a precondition to his leprosy's leaving him.[10] The purity sought after by obedience to the Law was unattainable to the leper unless God willed it. He must literally be purified by God to be cleansed, thus giving rise to the belief that he had truly repented.[11]

A leper bore the emblems of death (see Leviticus 13:45) and was literally mourned as if he were dead. Contact with a leper meant defilement, and the cleansing procedures were the same as when defiled by a dead body (see Numbers 19:6; Leviticus 14:4—7). David purged himself of spiritual leprosy with this cleansing procedure (see Psalm 51:7).

God on occasion used leprosy to punish those who sinned against his divine government. When Miriam spoke against Moses, she was smitten and "became leprous, white as snow" (see Numbers 12:1-10); Uzziah was smitten because he did not remove the "high places" where the "people sacrificed and burnt incense" (see 2 Kings 15:4—5); and Gehazi was cursed with the disease of Naaman for his evil before the Lord (see 2 Kings 5:27).

There could be no better way for the Lord of life to show that his mercy, love, and kingdom were extended to all than to heal the leper.

The Cleansing of the Leper

Mark 1:40—45

40. And there came a leper to him, beseeching him, and kneeling down to him, and saying unto him, If thou wilt, thou canst make me clean.

41. And Jesus, moved with compassion, put forth his hand, and touched him, and saith unto him, I will; be thou clean.

42. And as soon as he had spoken, immediately the leprosy departed from him, and he was cleansed.

43. And he straitly charged him, and forthwith sent him away;

44. And saith unto him, See thou say nothing to any man: but go thy way, shew thyself to the priest, and offer for thy cleansing those things which Moses commanded, for a testimony unto them.

45. But he went out, and began to publish it much, and to blaze abroad the matter, insomuch that Jesus

could no more openly enter
into the city, but was
without in desert places: and

they came to him from
every quarter.

Cross-references:

Matthew 8:1—4   Luke 5:12—16

A man "full of leprosy" came to Jesus and requested a miracle. His belief in the Lord was explicit. He did not ask to be made clean, but stated, "If thou wilt, thou canst make me clean." Here was a simple, open confession of faith, perhaps the first such confession in the Lord's public ministry. He believed that Jesus could heal him; his question was whether Jesus *would* heal him.

The request touched the heart of Jesus, and he "was moved with compassion." He put forth his hand and touched the leper, answering, "I will; be thou clean. And as soon as he had spoken, immediately the leprosy departed from him, and he was cleansed." The Lord had extended his power and healed the leper, but the miracle's significance went much deeper.

To the Jews the leper represented the most filthy of mankind. To touch him or be touched by him made one immediately unclean in the Levitical sense, yet Jesus simply reached out and touched him. In the touching and healing can be seen the purity and life offered by the kingdom of God. Jesus did not become unclean; rather, the man became clean.

The stories of Moses and the burning bush and Peter's dream of the sheet with food upon it represent a like principle. As Moses approached the bush, God spoke unto him: "put off thy shoes from off thy feet, for the place whereon thou standest is holy ground" (Exodus 3:5). The ground itself was not holy; God's presence made it holy.

Peter's vision occurred as he rested, awaiting dinner. In his vision a sheet, knitted "at the four corners," was let down, and all manner of meat was on it, including that which was forbidden under the Mosaic law. Peter was commanded to arise and "kill, and eat." He refused because the food was "common or unclean." The voice of God then attested to Peter, "What God hath cleansed, that call not thou common." The vision directed Peter concerning gentile membership in the kingdom of God; shortly thereafter, Cornelius and his house were admitted to the Church. (See Acts 10:11–20.) Here it was the same. What God had cleansed could not be declared unclean.

Jesus did not need to touch the leper to heal him, but by his touch and through this miracle he declared himself the Messiah, opened the kingdom to all, and abrogated Judaism henceforth.[12]

Two instructions were now given the leper. First, he was to "say nothing to any man"; and second, he was to show himself to the priest, thus complying with the cleansing requirements of the Mosaic Law. Judaism was in apostasy, yet the Mosaic Law was still in force. Jesus would not replace it until every "jot and tittle" had been fulfilled. Showing himself to the priest was not a requirement for Jesus' benefit but for the leper's. He had to comply with the Law before he could reenter the Jewish community.

Christ's first instruction ("say nothing to any man") is not as easily dealt with. On at least three other occasions Jesus left the recipient of a miracle with a similar instruction.[13] No immediate reason for such an instruction is given in the scriptures, but knowing that the Lord's primary concern is for all men to attain his kingdom, consider the following.

The effect upon the individual. Jesus gave this instruction upon four recorded occasions, and in each instance it was virtually impossible to fulfill. In this case, the leper must publicly declare his cleansing; and certainly family members, friends, and associates would know that he was now clean. All would question him concerning his healing, for they believed that a leper could only be cleansed by miraculous intervention.[14] Similarly, the two blind in the house were known to be blind (see chapter 15). They had shouted after Jesus and followed him into the house. The miracle could not be hidden, for they went into the house blind and came out seeing. Yet they were instructed to tell no one. In the raising of the daughter of Jairus (see chapter 8), all who were there and who had come with Jesus knew that the daughter had died, yet they saw her alive again. The healing of the deaf and dumb man (see chapter 16) stood amidst a multitude of miracles. Many had been healed, and the multitude present acknowledged that Jesus had "done all things well." How can such a miracle be kept a secret?

The Lord's instruction was apparently not meant to be a literal ban on all communication concerning the miracle. Rather, it cautioned the recipient on how he should speak of the miracle. Further, it focused attention on Jesus as the Messiah. Those healed were not to glory in the miracle. The Lord knew the personality and feelings of the recipients. Perhaps if they focused on the temporal results, reveling in the miracle itself, they might jeopardize the spiritual offering of the kingdom of God.

Only Mark emphasizes the leper's reaction in this miracle. Although Luke acknowledges that the miracle increased Christ's fame, he does not attribute it to the leper. Due to the joy the leper experienced at his healing, he probably found it difficult to remain silent. Although the immediate effect is recorded by Mark, the total effect upon the leper's life thereafter is not recorded in the scriptures.

The effect upon the immediate community. In the cleansing of the leper, the miracle's public effect was so overwhelming that Jesus could "no more openly enter into the city." The publicity brought great multitudes to hear him and to be healed by him. The emphasis of the multitude was, undoubtedly, on the temporal healing, and not on the spiritual blessing. The excitement sensationalized the Lord's healing powers rather than glorified his mission and kingdom. The Lord undoubtedly knew what effect the publicizing of the miracle would have upon the community in each case where the instruction, "Tell no one," was given. His miraculous powers were not just an appeal to the feelings and emotions of those who witnessed them, but were intended to be lodged in understanding and loving hearts. His desire, as always, was that all mankind would come unto him, repent, be baptized, and receive of his kingdom.

The Cleansing of Ten Lepers

Luke 17:12–19

12. And as he entered into a certain village, there met him ten men that were lepers, which stood afar off:

13. And they lifted up their voices, and said, Jesus, Master, have mercy on us.

14. And when he saw them, he said unto them, Go shew yourselves unto the

priests. And it came to pass, that, as they went, they were cleansed.

15. And one of them, when he saw that he was healed, turned back, and with a loud voice glorified God,

16. And fell down on his face at his feet, giving him thanks: and he was a Samaritan.

17. And Jesus answering said, Were there not ten cleansed? but where are the nine?

18. There are not found that returned to give glory to God, save this stranger.

19. And he said unto him, Arise, go thy way: thy faith hath made thee whole.

Luke records that as Jesus entered a certain village he encountered ten lepers. One is known to be a Samaritan and the other nine have always been assumed to be Jews.[15] Lepers could mingle and associate with each other, but with no one else. They heard that Jesus was coming and called after him, begging for his mercy. He immediately extended it. "Go shew yourselves unto the priests," he said. His instruction implied that the blessing had been granted, even though the miracle had not yet taken place. All ten believed that they would be healed, for they immediately left to comply with the Levitical Law; as they hurried to the priest, they were cleansed.

These men had the faith necessary to do as they were instructed, and the healing that took place witnessed not only their faith but the Lord's capacity as a healer. However, only one leper recognized who the healer was. As the healing took place, the Samaritan stopped and returned to Jesus, falling at the Lord's feet and giving thanks. Jesus acknowledged him and asked, "Were there not ten cleansed?" The other nine, in the joy of their temporal healing, had lost this opportunity for added spiritual growth; they were not to be found.[16] "Go thy way," Jesus stated. "Thy faith hath made thee whole." The Samaritan now received the added spiritual blessing the nine had missed. All ten had enough faith to go at his bidding and be healed; only one had enough faith to return and give thanks and glory to the healer.

This miracle is a perfect example of the universal charity that Jesus taught his disciples. The healed leper was a Samaritan, to the Jews a heathen from a hated race, yet he received the Lord's blessings, both physically and spiritually. "The occurrence must have impressed the Apostles as another evidence of acceptability and possible excellence on the part of aliens, to the disparagement of Jewish claims of superiority irrespective of merit."[17]

Finally, this incident provides a great object lesson on miracles. The miracle was simple and quick. There was no extensive test of faith or development of belief. The lepers requested the miracle and immediately received it. The ten lepers did not know that Jesus was the Messiah; they only believed that he could heal them. To the nine, once the blessing had been granted, the goal had been attained; but to the Samaritan, the healing was only the road to his goal. The healing brought joy and happiness to all the lepers, for it ended their misery. They rejoiced, and in that joy proceeded to comply with the Law and return to normal society. Nine were satisfied with a physical healing and did not see past it; the Samaritan saw past the temporal blessing and seized the opportunity for spiritual growth.

By healing the lepers Jesus extended his compassion to all, opened wide the doors of his kingdom, and abrogated Jewish exclusiveness forever.[18]

That the Blind May See 15

15

Spiritual Blindness

As were the lepers, the blind were considered "dead" by the Talmud,[1] even though they were treated with special kindness and mercy. Blindness had a special, symbolic meaning concerning the spiritual condition of Israel. It symbolized moral and spiritual decay and apostasy.[2] The Pharisees and scribes were offended at the teachings of Jesus. The Lord responded to their offense by instructing the disciples, "Let them alone: they be blind leaders of the blind. And if the blind lead the blind, both shall fall into the ditch" (Matthew 15:14). By healing the blind, Jesus symbolically testified to the Jews that he was offering them relief from their spiritual blindness and granting them new light.

That physical blindness and spiritual sight were associated is attested to in the Old Testament, where the Lord emphasized that disobedience to his commandments resulted in spiritual darkness. Moses summarized the cursings for disobedience to the Law in Deuteronomy: "If thou wilt not hearken unto the voice of the Lord thy God, to observe to do all his commandments and his statutes which I command thee this day; . . . all these curses shall come upon thee, and overtake thee" (Deuteronomy 28:15). The list of specific curses followed. Then Moses described Israel's disobedient condition as a people that "grope at noonday, as the blind gropeth in darkness" (Deuteronomy 28:29).

Isaiah used the analogy to describe the spiritual darkness of the last days. He said, "We grope for the wall like the blind, and we grope as if we had no eyes: we stumble at noonday as in the night; we are in desolate places as dead men" (Isaiah 59:10). When Job discussed his beleaguered condition with his friends and associates, he compared those without God's light to those who "grope in the dark without light, and he maketh them to stagger like a drunken man" (see Job 12:25). Zephaniah described this spiritual darkness clearly. He said of the Lord's reaction to those who would neither heed nor accept his word, "And I will bring distress upon men, that they shall walk like blind men, because they have sinned against the Lord" (Zephaniah 1:17).

Blindness indicated a loss of the spiritual light God had given. Thus, to be healed meant deliverance from sin and the removal of this spiritual blindness (see Isaiah 29:18; Ephesians 5:8). Jesus declared openly that he was "the light of the world" (John 8:12). Through him their spiritual blindness would be taken away. The healings of the blind were the embodiment of that testimony.

The Two Blind in the House

Matthew 9:27–31

27. And when Jesus departed thence, two blind men followed him, crying, and saying, Thou Son of David, have mercy on us.

28. And when he was come into the house, the blind men came to him: and Jesus saith unto them, Believe ye that I am able to do this? They said unto him, Yea, Lord.

29. Then touched he their eyes, saying, According to your faith be it unto you.

30. And their eyes were opened; and Jesus straitly charged them, saying, See that no man know it.

31. But they, when they were departed, spread abroad his fame in all that country.

Cross-reference:

JST Matthew 9:36

The Blind at Jericho

Luke 18:35—43

35. And it came to pass, that as he was come nigh unto Jericho, a certain blind man sat by the way side begging:

36. And hearing the multitude pass by, he asked what it meant.

37. And they told him, that Jesus of Nazareth passeth by.

38. And he cried, saying, Jesus, thou Son of David, have mercy on me.

39. And they which went before rebuked him, that he should hold his peace: but he cried so much the more, Thou Son of David, have mercy on me.

40. And Jesus stood, and commanded him to be brought unto him: and when he was come near, he asked him,

41. Saying, What wilt thou that I shall do unto thee? And he said, Lord, that I may receive my sight.

42. And Jesus said unto him, Receive thy sight: thy faith hath saved thee.

43. And immediately he received his sight, and followed him, glorifying God: and all the people, when they saw it, gave praise unto God.

Cross-references:

Matthew 20:29—34   Mark 10:46—52

Since these two miracles are very similar they will here be discussed together. Further, they will be treated topically rather than sequentially.

The divergence between the synoptic accounts. Only Matthew records both miracles. I offer the suggestion that the differences between Matthew and the other two Synoptics are perhaps caused by the duplicating or superimposing in Matthew's Jericho miracle of facts from his chapter 9 miracle. (The difficulties of this area in Matthew chapter 9 have been discussed before —see chapter 3—and need not be taken up again here.) With this interpretation, the facts of the two Matthew miracles would be coordinated in favor of the chapter 9 miracle. This would leave the balance of the facts describing the Jericho miracle in agreement with Mark and Luke. Thus there would be two blind men in the miracle in chapter 9 (the two blind men in the house) and only one in the Jericho miracle (whom Mark names Bartimaeus). Jesus touched the eyes of the blind in the chapter 9 miracle, but not in the Jericho miracle. It is not possible to determine whether Jesus performed the miracle upon entering (Luke) or exiting (Matthew and Mark) Jericho.

The blind men's unique request and their persistence. These were requested miracles. The blind were disadvantaged compared with the other sick people that came to Jesus requesting help. They did not have freedom of movement and had to be told when Jesus was present. Once these blind men knew Jesus was in their vicinity they would not let the opportunity pass. They cried after him, for that was the only way they could attract his attention. They were not ashamed of their desire, and even though Jesus seemed at first to ignore them, they would not be still. In Matthew, chapter 9, they followed him into a house to further petition their cause; in the Jericho miracle the multitude surrounding Jesus wanted to quiet them, but they "cried so much the more," for it was their only chance. In both circumstances it is evident that Jesus was known to them, and once the opportunity to be healed presented itself, they would not be denied. Their cry for help and their persistence demonstrated their faith in his power to restore their sight.

The title used to address Jesus; i.e., the Son of David. It is unlikely that these blind men recognized Jesus as the Messiah. They probably addressed him in this manner as a title of homage. In their cry for help was "the hope" of the Messiah, expressed in a common form of address of the time,[3] rather than a sure knowledge or belief that he was the awaited Savior.[4] Their cry did evidence, however, that they hoped and believed that he could

and would heal them. They petitioned for the Lord's mercy, and
when questioned concerning their desire their response was direct
and to the point: they wanted their sight restored. After receiving
the blessing they desired, they followed and praised the Lord.
Only in the title they used to address him is there an indication of
anything other than a temporal desire for the healing of their
blindness. The title itself was not denied by Jesus; he was the Son
of David.

The Lord's question. In the Lord's question and action lay a
source of help to those who could not see. In terms of the men's
immediate need it was redundant for Jesus to ask what the blind
men wanted, for what they wanted was obvious. But the question allowed a strengthening of the faith first demonstrated by
their cry for help. Jesus ignored their initial request, and by so
doing witnessed their determination. His next actions encouraged
that persistent desire. He "stood" or stopped to talk with the man
in the Jericho miracle, and he received the blind into the house in
the chapter 9 miracle. Such actions could only have increased the
confidence of the blind. In the Jericho miracle, the blind man
eagerly responded to his question by answering that he wanted to
receive his sight; in the chapter 9 miracle, the blind acknowledged
their belief that the Lord could perform the miracle. Thus the
Lord helped them obtain their desire by helping them increase
their faith.

The crowd's reaction in the Jericho miracle. The crowd's
reaction in this miracle is interesting. The blind man heard the
crowd coming and asked who was causing so much excitement.
He was eagerly told that Jesus of Nazareth was passing by. The
blind man immediately began shouting after Jesus to gain his
attention. The people "rebuked him, that he should hold his
peace." Perhaps they did not want the Master to be interrupted
or disturbed. Jesus often taught as he walked, and the crowd may
have been trying to hear him. The disciples had, on a previous
occasion, attempted to restrain little children from coming to the
Master (see Mark 10:13–14). On another occasion, when Jesus
initially ignored the plea of the Syrophenician woman, the
disciples attempted to send her away to silence her (see Matthew
15:22–23). But now Jesus stopped and called for the man, and
the crowd quickly changed its attitude. "Be of good comfort. . . ;

he calleth thee," they said. But the crowd remained spiritually blind. They had tried to silence the one whose sight was dead, and who was, in their minds, spiritually dead as well; but the Light of the world would have it otherwise and gave him his sight.

The instruction to tell no one. This material was previously discussed in detail (see chapter 15) and need not be reiterated here except to determine its importance in this particular situation. The blind men were undoubtedly well known in the area. They cried after Jesus, followed the crowd, and then went with the Lord into the house. They went in blind, but they came forth seeing.

It was virtually impossible to avoid publicizing this miracle. The Lord would have known this, but his admonition sought to direct the attention of the healed to the miracle's source rather than to their joy over its temporal effects. The Lord was teaching his Messianic identity.[5] This realization would best come to the blind men through contemplation and following the Master, not by demonstrating their newly regained sight. However, the men chose to "spread abroad his fame."[6]

These two miracles testified of Jesus as the Light of the world, and seemingly were directed at blind Israel. Isaiah had prophesied, "See ye indeed, but perceive not . . . shut their eyes; lest they see with their eyes, . . . and convert, and be healed." (Isaiah 6:9—10.) After the parable of the sower the Lord said of them (the Pharisees and scribes), "seeing [they] see not; . . . and their eyes they have closed" (see Matthew 13:13, 15). The Light of the world had come so that the blind, both the physically blind and the spiritually blind, might see.

Part Seven

Faith and
Miracles

Increasing Faith Through Miracles

16

One Deaf and Dumb

Mark 7:31—37

31. And again, departing from the coasts of Tyre and Sidon, he came unto the sea of Galilee, through the midst of the coasts of Decapolis.

32. And they bring unto him one that was deaf, and had an impediment in his speech; and they beseech him to put his hand upon him.

33. And he took him aside from the multitude, and put his fingers into his ears, and he spit, and touched his tongue;

34. And looking up to heaven, he sighed, and saith unto him, Ephphatha, that is, Be opened.

35. And straightway his ears were opened, and the string of his tongue was loosed, and he spake plain.

36. And he charged them that they should tell no man: but the more he charged them, so much the more a great deal they published it;

37. And were beyond measure astonished, saying, He hath done all things well: he maketh both the deaf to hear, and the dumb to speak.

This miracle occurs while Jesus is by the coasts of Decapolis. It is given to a people classified as heathen and Gentiles.[1] Only Mark records it, and it occurs some time between the raising of the daughter of Jairus and the feeding of the four thousand. The heathen did not have Israel's history and did not believe in or look forward to a Messiah.

After the miracle involving the daughter of the Syrophenician woman, Christ's fame spread rapidly. As a result, many came to him to be healed (see Matthew 15:29—30), their faith being based on the miracles Jesus performed. As more came, their faith increased as they witnessed the continuous healing of all the sick and disabled in the multitude. The miracle of the deaf and dumb man was one from this multitude of miracles.

A man was brought to Jesus to be healed. He was described as being deaf and dumb with an impediment of speech. The Lord "took him aside from the multitude" to perform the miracle. This was to be a miracle of instruction for the one deaf and dumb and the Twelve, not for the multitude in general. The Lord then performed this miracle in a most peculiar manner, and "we are disposed to regard this as peculiar to the healing of Gentiles."[2]

First, he carefully put his fingers in the man's ears. This physical act had nothing to do with the healing process itself, but to the man it may have seemed that he was thrusting in his fingers to make way for the sound.[3] The Lord's actions were presumably a sign that he was removing the man's deafness. Jesus then spit (probably upon his fingers) and touched the man's tongue. Again it was a sign, symbolizing the healing of the man's speech impediment. Each act of the Lord "seemed a fresh incitement to his faith"[4] and was a manifestation solely for the man's benefit. He completed the healing process with a vocal command. He looked up to heaven and sighed. The sigh may have been an expression of concern for these heathen or evidence of his compassion and deep concern for their physical and spiritual problems. He spoke the word "Ephphatha," which Mark interpreted as "Be opened." The signs of healing that Jesus had given were now confirmed. The command was obeyed, and the man both heard and spoke clearly.

Jesus next admonished both the man and those that had brought him to "tell no man," but they could not be silent. Mark records that "the more he charged them, so much the more a great deal they published it." The man did not obey Christ's admonition, but it appears that in his disobedience additional belief in Jesus was generated. He could not contain his joy, but "published it." The reaction of the community was favorable, for they concluded that "he hath done all things well."

It appears that the more miracles the Gentiles saw, the more readily they accepted Christ's teachings. Thus they might come to understand him as the Messiah. Later teachings could build on this foundation and increase their spiritual enlightenment. They would be taught the words of life and salvation. No doubt the man who had been deaf and dumb would also receive the Lord's teachings. His healing would have prepared him to receive and understand Christ's words, and his faith would have been expanded as a result of the Lord's miraculous power.

One Blind at Bethsaida

Mark 8:22—26

22. And he cometh to Bethsaida; and they bring a blind man unto him, and besought him to touch him.

23. And he took the blind man by the hand, and led him out of the town; and when he had spit on his eyes, and put his hands upon him, he asked him if he saw ought.

24. And he looked up, and said, I see men as trees, walking.

25. After that he put his hands again upon his eyes, and made him look up: and he was restored, and saw every man clearly.

26. And he sent him away to his house, saying, Neither go into the town, nor tell it to any in the town.

Cross-reference:

JST Mark 8:27

Mark records that the blind man in this miracle was brought to Jesus in Bethsaida-Julias, a Gentile city filled with heathenism and Hellenism.[5] Since this miracle and the healing of the deaf and dumb man are so similar in approach and style, it seems logical to assume that this blind man was a heathen also.[6] The individuals who brought the man to Jesus petitioned him to touch him, as did those who accompanied the deaf and dumb man. Again, as in the previous miracle, the blind man does not speak in his own behalf before the miracle begins.

This is the only recorded instance where Jesus healed someone by stages. He took the man by the hand and led him outside the town. This, also, was not a miracle for exhibition, but for the blind man, his companions, and the Twelve. Upon arriving at a private area, Jesus "spit on his eyes," and "put his hands upon him." This procedure was uniquely tailored to this blind man, that he might gain confidence in his healer.[7] As with those used on the deaf and dumb man, apart from the priesthood ordinance of the laying on of hands such procedures had nothing to do with the Lord's power to heal, but were performed so that the blind man could believe in the person performing the healing.[8] At this point the Lord asked the blind man if he could see, and his strange response was, "I see men as trees, walking." He could not see normally, but apparently was only partially cured. Jesus then put his hands on his eyes again and "made him look up: and he was restored, and saw every man clearly." He then instructed the man to go to his house, and not into the city. He was not to tell "it to any in the town." This instruction was probably given to best accommodate the man's future spiritual growth, and the growth of those he would come in contact with (see chapter 14). No information is given on the outcome of the instruction, and it can be assumed that the man followed the Lord's directions.

Mark gives no explanation for the gradual healing the Lord performed on this occasion. The procedures Christ used were undoubtedly intended to strengthen the blind man's faith as step by step the Lord led him through the miracle, and step by step his faith and knowledge of the Savior increased.

Summary

The Lord used his miracles for many purposes, including the teaching and nurturing of faith. The healing of the deaf and dumb man and the one blind at Bethsaida seem to have been recorded to specifically illustrate this purpose. Both miracles were requested. From the evidence available, both men were heathen, ready believers in mysticism and miracles. Yet the Lord's peculiar method of healing led them away from their heathen gods and mystical powers. Throughout the healing process Christ strengthened their faith and led them step by step to a stronger belief in him. They came to him with a temporal need, requesting a temporal blessing. He adapted their cure to fit their spiritual needs, that he might lead them beyond the temporal blessing to the spiritual opportunity.

The Apostles Instructed in Faith Through Miracles

The Dumb Lunatic Child

Mark 9:14—29

14. And when he came to his disciples, he saw a great multitude about them, and the scribes questioning with them.

15. And straightway all the people, when they beheld him, were greatly amazed and, running to him saluted him.

16. And he asked the scribes, What question ye with them?

17. And one of the multitude answered and said, Master, I have brought unto thee my son, which hath a dumb spirit;

18. And wheresoever he taketh him, he teareth him: and he foameth, and gnasheth with his teeth, and pineth away: and I spake to thy disciples that they should cast him out; and they could not.

19. He answereth him, and saith, O faithless generation, how long shall I be with you? how long shall I suffer you? bring him unto me.

20. And they brought him unto him: and when he saw him, straightway the spirit tare him; and he fell

on the ground, and wallowed foaming.

21. And he asked his father, How long is it ago since this came unto him? And he said, Of a child.

22. And ofttimes it hath cast him into the fire, and into the waters, to destroy him: but if thou canst do any thing, have compassion on us, and help us.

23. Jesus said unto him, If thou canst believe, all things are possible to him that believeth.

24. And straightway the father of the child cried out, and said with tears, Lord, I believe; help thou mine unbelief.

25. When Jesus saw that the people came running together, he rebuked the foul spirit, saying unto him, Thou dumb and deaf spirit, I charge thee, come out of him, and enter no more into him.

26. And the spirit cried, and rent him sore, and came out of him: and he was as one dead; insomuch that many said, He is dead.

27. But Jesus took him by the hand, and lifted him up; and he arose.

28. And when he was come into the house, his disciples asked him privately, Why could not we cast him out?

29. And he said unto them, This kind can come forth by nothing, but by prayer and fasting.

Cross-references:

Matthew 17:14—21   Luke 9:37—43   JST Mark 9:15, 20

This is one of the most public of Jesus' miracles. Each miracle has its place in the Lord's teachings, but on the subject of faith this miracle is outstanding. While it is recorded by all three Synoptics, Mark is used here as the primary text.

The miracle initially benefited only one young boy, but its influence went far beyond that physical healing. Its powerful message taught the principle of faith to the multitude, to the boy's father, and especially to the Twelve. It taught the relationship between the worlds of Christ and of Satan and between belief and unbelief; and it demonstrated whether faith is precedent or antecedent to blessings. It also afforded a glimpse into Jesus' personal character.

Prior to this miracle Jesus was on the Mount of Transfiguration with Peter, James, and John. These Apostles witnessed the Lord's transfiguration and heard the Father's testimony of his Son's divinity. At the conclusion of this exalting, spiritual experience, the four came down from the Mount and interrupted a dispute between the scribes and the other nine Apostles. The nine had failed to perform a miracle. A young boy had been brought to them by his father to have an evil spirit cast out. He had come in search of Jesus, but when Jesus could not be found, he presented the child to the nine and requested them to heal him. Their failure resulted in the dispute.

No detail is given of this argument, but the scribes undoubtedly relished the fact that the nine Apostles could not perform this healing. Their elation was to be short lived, however. As Jesus approached the disputing parties he immediately removed the burden of conversation from the nine Apostles and assumed it himself. "What question ye with them?" he asked. No response came from the scribes or the nine Apostles. The father of the afflicted boy stepped forward, described his son's illness, and disclosed that the nine could not cast out the evil spirit.

"O faithless generation," Jesus exclaimed. His words were a rebuke to them all: to the scribes for contending with the nine and lacking faith in the Son of God; to the father for his wavering faith; to the multitude for their avid interest in seeing miracles performed, and their blindness in recognizing the Messiah; and to the nine Apostles, because they had allowed their faith to weaken even though they had specifically been given the power to heal and cast out devils (see Matthew 10:1, 8). Jesus then declared, "How long shall I be with you?" His words bemoaned the fact that he would not be with the Apostles much longer, and yet they still seemed to lack faith in him and his authority. He questioned, "How long shall I suffer you?" The failure of the nine Apostles to cure the dumb lunatic child and the contending scribes undoubtedly aroused doubt in the minds of the multitude. Christ's arrival had caused great excitement, and the crowd was "greatly amazed" to see him.[1] Jesus commanded that the child be brought to him, and the eager crowd pressed close to see what would happen.

As the child approached Jesus, the evil spirit that possessed him attacked him anew, causing him to fall to the ground and foam at the mouth. Jesus asked the father how long the boy had been ill. The father indicated that he had suffered since childhood, and he explained the history of the malady. The Lord's presence and his question produced the desired effect upon the father; the love he had for his only son subdued his doubt. He asked for the Lord's help, but the phrasing of his request evidenced lingering apprehension. He pleaded with the Lord as he asked, "If thou canst do any thing, have compassion on us, and help us." The "if" conveyed the doubt the father still held.

Although unwittingly used, the word may have recalled to Christ his encounter with Satan when the devil tempted him. Satan's approach was cleverly couched in such a manner as to tempt Jesus to question his ability, his mission, and his relationship with the Father. "If thou be the Son of God," the devil had said as he tempted him (see Matthew 4:3, 6).

Jesus now began teaching faith to the father, the Apostles, and all the multitude. To the father he declared, "If thou canst believe, all things are possible to him that believeth."

The man cried out to the Lord, and "with tears" in his eyes said, "Lord, I believe; help thou mine unbelief." He had again mustered that same hope and belief that had originally brought him in search of Jesus. But now, and most important, the father recognized his limited faith and cried for help; not just help to cure his son, but help to increase his faith in the Lord.[2]

When Jesus saw that the multitude was running to see what was happening, he rebuked the evil spirit, charging it to come out and "enter no more into him." The evil spirit cried out, and "rent him sore" as it left him. The boy appeared dead but was raised up by the Lord and given to the father.

Jesus returned to the house with the Twelve, and the nine Apostles asked why they could not cast out the evil spirit. Jesus responded that "this kind can come forth by nothing, but by prayer and fasting." This was the key to the miracle for the Apostles. They had failed because of unbelief. It was the source of their weakness and of all weakness where divine intervention is concerned.[3] It was not the Lord's ability that was in question,

but their own. As they watched, the Master had easily cast out
the evil spirit, even though they could not. In their failure Christ
prescribed a method that would help keep their faith constant
and vital—prayer and fasting!

This miracle was a lesson to the Twelve on the principles of
belief and unbelief. By their ordination to the Apostleship, they
had been given the power to perform such healings as this one,
but its use depended upon their complete faith in the Lord. All
men stand in the same position and need constant assurance that
divine help will be forthcoming to fortify us against unbelief.

The possession of this afflicted boy dated from childhood. Its
description evidenced the powerful control the evil spirit had
over him. But more than this, when they brought the boy to
Jesus, the spirit violently rebelled. It "straightway" forced him to
the ground, "tare him," and caused him to foam at the mouth.
When Jesus commanded the spirit to leave the boy, it "cried, and
rent him sore," before coming out of him. The possession was so
overpowering that after leaving the boy's body, he "was as one
dead."

The two kingdoms, Christ's and the devil's, had once again
come together in open conflict. Jesus is the head of his kingdom,
and others (such as the Twelve) have designated authority in it.
The devil is the head of his kingdom, and others have authority
under him.[4] Jesus described the spirit as "this kind," which might
indicate that this particular evil spirit was one with authority. To
the Lord of all it was but a simple task to cast him out, for the evil
spirit was bound to obey him. But the nine, with their doubts and
weakened faith, could not maintain the spiritual strength that
would allow them to exercise the power Jesus did, and so they
failed. Yet they learned from this failure.

An interesting example in the book of Acts illustrates this
principle. After explaining that Paul wrought special miracles,
the scripture reports that "certain of the vagabond Jews, exor-
cists," attempted to cast out evil spirits. They "adjured" them in
the name of "Jesus whom Paul preacheth" to come out. The
spirits communicated with the Jews and answered, "Jesus I know,
and Paul I know; but who are ye?" The evil spirits then attacked
them, and they fled "naked and wounded." The spirits knew and

recognized proper authority when it was exercised with proper faith. (See Acts 19:13—16.)

Several principles concerning faith are taught by this miracle:

1. Faith in Jesus is personal, and it may increase or decrease depending upon the individual and his reaction to a given circumstance.

2. The use of Jesus' divine authority and power, even when properly held, is dependent upon individual faith.

3. One procedure for increasing and renewing faith in him is prayer and fasting.

4. When faith and belief have been replaced by doubt and disbelief, a personal renewal is necessary prior to Christ's intervention and assistance.

5. The Lord will always aid and assist those who believe in him and rely on his divine compassion and mercy.

6. Jesus, by analogy, taught that even an amount of faith as small as the grain of mustard seed could move mountains. By this example, he emphasized that it was not the quantity of faith that was important, but the quality. All things are possible as a result of unwavering faith.

7. Perfect faith is not required to receive God's blessings. Miracles can be received by those of weak or almost nonexistent faith, the miracle being used as a teaching tool to build faith.[5] This tool would be used repeatedly by the Apostles (see Acts 1:14; 9:9; 10:9, 30; 13:2—3; 14:23).

Resolving Personal Problems

The Water to Wine

John 2:1–11

1. And the third day there was a marriage in Cana of Galilee; and the mother of Jesus was there:

2. And both Jesus was called, and his disciples, to the marriage.

3. And when they wanted wine, the mother of Jesus saith unto him, They have no wine.

4. Jesus saith unto her, Woman, what have I to do with thee? mine hour is not yet come.

5. His mother saith unto the servants, Whatsoever he saith unto you, do it.

6. And there were set there six waterpots of stone, after the manner of the purifying of the Jews, containing two or three firkins apiece.

7. Jesus saith unto them, Fill the waterpots with water. And they filled them up to the brim.

8. And he saith unto them, Draw out now, and bear unto the governor of the feast. And they bare it.

9. When the ruler of the feast had tasted the water that was made wine, and knew not whence it was: (but the servants which drew

the water knew;) the governor of the feast called the bridegroom,

10. And saith unto him, Every man at the beginning doth set forth good wine; and when men have well drunk, then that which is worse: but thou hast kept the good wine until now.

11. This beginning of miracles did Jesus in Cana of Galilee, and manifested forth his glory; and his disciples believed on him.

Cross-reference:

JST John 2:4, 11

The miracles in this chapter deal with personal problems. The miracle of turning the water to wine is reported as the "beginning of miracles." It is a miracle of declaration, kindness, joy, and testimony. It was performed in Cana of Galilee at a marriage feast. Jesus and his disciples had been invited to join the festivities. John is the only Gospel writer that reports the miracle. Prior to the miracle John records his call, and that of Peter, Andrew, Philip, and Nathanael; therefore, it is assumed that these five were present with Jesus on this occasion.

Marriage was a sacred event to the Jews. It symbolized the union of God with Israel,[1] and entrance into matrimony was thought to carry with it a forgiveness of sin.[2] The sacredness of the marriage covenant had almost been elevated to the level of a sacrament,[3] and the pious even fasted before it.[4]

Nothing is known about the participants in this wedding. It has been assumed that either the bride or the bridegroom was of Jesus' immediate family, perhaps a brother, sister, or nephew. This assumption is made because of the prominence of Mary, the mother of Jesus, in the order of the festivities.[5]

The Lord's participation in this event demonstrated his approval and endorsement of marriage and the propriety of social interaction.[6] His life was not to be as that of John the Baptist—a life withdrawn from the paths of other men and their social habits. Jesus was destined to be among men, to share their joys, sorrows, and social engagements, and to enter into their family life. Through his involvement, men's lives would be purified and elevated to a higher spiritual level.[7]

Jesus was the second of two witnesses who came in a manner
that Israel would recognize. John the Baptist was the first witness,
and like the great prophets of the desert (Elijah and Elisha), he
exemplified the ascetic or highest form of Jewish religious life.

> [John] had spent his days in penitential austerity and
> wilderness seclusion; had drunk no wine, had eaten no
> pleasant food, and had kept apart from human affairs and
> relationships. But a new and higher ideal of religion was now
> to be introduced. Jesus [the second witness to Israel] came to
> spiritualize the humblest duties of life, and sanctify its
> simplest incidents, so as to enoble it as a whole. Henceforth,
> pleasures and enjoyments were not to be shunned as unholy;
> religion was not to thrive on the mortification of every
> human instinct, and the repression of every cheerful emotion.
> It would mix with the crowd of men, affect no singularity,
> take part in the innocent festivities of life, interest itself in
> whatever interested men at large, and yet, amidst all, remain
> consecrated and pure; in the world, by sympathy and active
> brotherhood, but not of it; human in its outward form, but
> heavenly in its elevation and spirit.[8]

Jesus came to Israel in the tradition of Isaiah, Jeremiah, and
Ezekiel. He was known to the Jews and participated in their customs and traditions.

As the wedding festivities progressed, need for a personal
miracle developed. There was a call for additional wine, and
none was available. Mary came to Jesus and told him of the
problem. What she wanted of Jesus is not specifically stated, but
it appears that she expected his assistance to solve her dilemma.[9]
No great catastrophe would have occurred without Jesus' intervention, but mockery and scorn would have come upon the
bridal couple if they had run out of wine. The Jewish traditions
had become so inflexible that failure to comply with them threatened disgrace on the family for life. The marriage feast was the
highest of social activities, and the tradition of the feast required
abundant wine.[10]

Thus, Mary petitioned her son for help with this personal
problem to avoid social disgrace. According to the King James
Version, the Lord's response was, "Woman, what have I to do
with thee, mine hour is not yet come." His response was not an

insult to his mother,[11] and in fact, the salutation "woman" was commonly used in that day. It denoted the "queenliest and most loved."[12] However, the Lord's answer appears to contain a mild rebuke similar to that response given to Mary when he was twelve years old and was found teaching in the temple (Luke 2:49). There the scripture reports that Mary did not understand his comments (Luke 2:50). In the current instance, the JST adds to the understanding of the event, translating the verse to read: "Woman, what wilt thou have me to do for thee? that will I do; for mine hour is not yet come" (JST John 2:4). Jesus would help his mother, but he reminded her that he was more than the son of Mary, he was the Son of God. By this time Jesus had already been baptized, received the Holy Ghost, been tempted in the wilderness by the devil, and called the first of his Apostles. His ministry had officially commenced; the tender, earthly relationship with his mother would not be forgotten, but his "business," his mission from the Father, was not primarily concerned with these earthly relationships and needs.[13]

It is evident that Mary took no offense, for she immediately instructed the servants to do as he bade them. Even though her problem was personal and confined to a social situation, she had complete confidence that he would assist her.

Jesus instructed the servants to fill six nearby pots with water. John is particular to note that the water pots were there according to custom, "after the manner of the purifying of the Jews."[14] After filling the pots with water, he instructed the servants to "draw out now, and bear unto the governor of the feast." The water had been made into wine, and the bridegroom was complimented for his generosity in keeping the "good wine" for last.

The Lord's act of consideration confirmed two principles involving divine intervention in personal lives: first, that requests for divine assistance can be made to resolve specific personal problems; and second, that such assistance will be granted to those with a firm belief in the Lord's ability to help them.

The miracle of turning the water to wine was completed without fanfare or public notice. But its circumstances have given rise to several questions.

Had Christ performed previous miracles? There is no scriptural evidence or testimony that Jesus performed any miracles prior to the official commencement of his ministry. The circumstances in this miracle, however, indicate that miracles may have been performed prior to turning the water to wine. Mary's request intimated that she knew Jesus had such capabilities, whether he had demonstrated them or not.[15] Jesus brought to the feast several men he had called to the Apostleship. The call of these men (Peter, Andrew, John, Nathanael, and Philip) was treated summarily by John (see John 1:37—49), yet there is evidence of Christ's using his miraculous abilities. When Nathanael was called, Jesus revealed that he saw him "under the fig tree" before Philip brought him to the Lord. There is additional evidence in the other Gospels that he had used his powers prior to the wedding at Cana. The miracle of the first draught of fish (see chapter 7) took place when Jesus called Peter, Andrew, James, and John as Apostles. It would, therefore, be reasonable to assume that changing water into wine was not the literal "beginning of miracles," but the first recorded by John. If previous miracles (i.e., previous to the commencement of Christ's ministry) had been performed, it would seem likely that they were performed in the privacy of his family and were not publicly known.

How was the water changed to wine? Historically there has been much speculation on this subject. Some writers have suggested that Jesus brought the wine and mixed it with the water. Others claim Mary brought it as a gift to Jesus, and he merely gave it to those at the feast.[16] Still others feel that it was a mere acceleration of the natural laws of nature.[17] Some reject the miracle altogether, because to them it was a miracle of luxury rather than one of beneficence.[18] All rational attempts at an explanation are fruitless. The Lord of heaven and earth could easily perform such a task, and speculation on the actual process is superfluous.

What was this wine? There has been some question raised as to whether Jesus drank fermented wine, or whether the wine was nonalcoholic. The scriptures clearly use the term "wine," and no attempt is made by the writers to exclude Christ from its general use. Many different types of wine were common during Christ's time.[19] Jesus undoubtedly drank the common beverages of his day, and the Mosaic Law did not prohibit Israelites in general from drinking wine. There were some specific situations in which wine was prohibited. Aaron and his sons were prohibited from drinking wine when they entered the tabernacle (see Leviticus 10:9). An individual who took the vow of a Nazarite was prohibited from using wine (see Numbers 6:1–3) along with many other restrictions (see Numbers 6:4–21). The mother of Samson was not a Nazarite, but she was commanded to observe the prohibitions of that order until Samson was born, for he was to be a Nazarite from birth (see Judges 13:4–5, 7).

Matthew reports a discussion Jesus had with his Apostles concerning the prophecies of his coming among the Jews. Jesus describes both John the Baptist and himself as the witnesses to Israel of the Messiah, and states, "John came neither eating nor drinking, and they say, He hath a devil. The Son of man came eating and drinking, and they say, Behold a man gluttonous, and a winebibber." (Matthew 11:18–19; see also Luke 7:33–34.) John the Baptist was raised as a Nazarite (see Luke 1:15), symbolizing the prophets of old in his witness of Christ. The Lord came among his people "eating and drinking" and participating in the Jews' daily activities.

Wedding celebrations could extend beyond a single day.[20] The comment of the governor of the feast that the best wine was usually served first, and "when men have well drunk, then that which is worse" was served, might lead some to speculate that at such feasts, overindulgence was tolerated. But such was not the case. The Lord would not have sanctioned such behavior, and definitely would not have augmented it by his miraculous service. The Jews knew the pros and cons of wine, and they held drunkenness in abhorrence. In Christ's household, this license would not have been allowed.[21] One of the popular parables of the time exemplified this principle. It stated:

> When Noah planted his vineyard, Satan came and asked him what he was doing? "Planting a vineyard," was the reply. "What is it for?" "Its fruits, green or dry, are sweet and pleasant: we make wine of it, which gladdens the heart." "I should like to have a hand in the planting," said Satan. "Good," replied Noah. Satan then brought a lamb, a lion, a sow, and an ape, killed them in the vineyard, and let their blood run into the roots of the vines. From this is come that a man

before he has taken wine, is simple as a lamb, which knows nothing, and is dumb before its shearers; when he has drunk moderately he grows a lion, and thinks there is not his like; if he drink too much, he turns a swine, and wallows in the mire; if he drink still more, he becomes a filthy ape, falling hither and thither, and knowing nothing of what he does.[22]

Jesus would no more have participated in the excessive use of wine or in drunkenness than in any other sin whose consequence would exclude the sinner from the kingdom of God (see 1 Corinthians 6:10).

Summary. This was not a public miracle, yet it would be publicized. The report indicates that the governor did not know the water had been made into wine—only the servants did. The miracle's primary purpose was to solve a personal problem. However, as in all miracles, the Lord used it as a teaching tool. John notes that Christ "manifested forth his glory; and his disciples believed on him." He had used his miraculous power on a work of mercy for his mother, but it instilled confirmation and trust in his disciples. He unveiled his glory before them, and it increased their growing faith.

Peter's Wife's Mother

Matthew 8:14–15

14. And when Jesus was come into Peter's house, he saw his wife's mother laid, and sick of a fever.

15. And he touched her hand, and the fever left her: and she arose, and ministered unto them.

Cross-references:

Mark 1:29–31   Luke 4:38–39

This was the second miracle performed to resolve a personal problem. Jesus was returning after healing the demoniac in the synagogue at Capernaum. He was accompanied by Peter, Andrew, James, and John. When they arrived at Simon Peter's house, they found his mother-in-law seriously ill with a fever (frequently translated from the Greek as "burning fever").[23] Peter and the others petitioned Jesus on her behalf that he might heal her. It was a completely natural petition. In view of the fact that Jesus had just compassionately healed a complete stranger, it was only logical that he should do likewise for one that loved him.

The Talmud prescribed a detailed cure for this precise problem. The afflicted person was told to "tie a knife wholly of iron by a braid of hair to a thornbush, and . . . repeat on successive days Exodus 3:2, 3, then verse 4, and finally verse 5, after which the bush is to be cut down, while a certain magical formula is pronounced."[24] Jesus merely took the woman by the hand and rebuked the fever with the power vested in him. She was healed instantly and completely, and arose immediately and "ministered unto them."

All three Synoptics record this miracle, but none detail or record any reaction to it. The miracle would have increased the faith of all who witnessed it, but not even this is mentioned. It seems its only purpose was to grant the righteous desire of a loved one, and the Lord freely gave of his love and compassion to assist with this personal problem.

The Coin in the Mouth of the Fish

Matthew 17:24—27

24. And when they were come to Capernaum, they that received tribute money came to Peter, and said, . Doth not your master pay tribute?

25. He saith, Yes. And when he was come into the house, Jesus prevented him, saying, What thinkest thou, Simon? of whom do the kings of the earth take custom or tribute? of their own children, or of strangers?

26. Peter saith unto him, Of strangers. Jesus saith unto him, Then are the children free.

27. Notwithstanding, lest we should offend them, go thou to the sea, and cast an hook, and take up the fish that first cometh up; and when thou hast opened his mouth, thou shalt find a piece of money: that take, and give unto them for me and thee.

Cross-reference:

JST Matthew 17:24

This last personal miracle is recorded by Matthew. It appears to have but one functional purpose — that of providing a solution to Peter's self-caused dilemma — but it is full of meaning though it is often overlooked.

The miracle revolves around the tribute money assessed as a tax for the temple. The tax was an annual one and was assessed upon every male Israelite over the age of twenty years, including proselytes and freed slaves. It was a tax of redemption from sin assessed under the Law of Moses, and was assessed to all in the same amount, whether rich or poor (see Exodus 30:13—16; 38:25—26).[25]

The collectors of this tax had the right to ask Peter, "Doth not your master pay tribute?" They also had the right to collect the fee. Priests and rabbis claimed an exemption from the tax,[26] and the phrasing of the tax collectors' question indicated that they did not know whether Jesus paid the tax or claimed the exemption.

The tax was used for the following items:

1. To purchase beasts for the temple sacrifices.

2. To pay copiers, bakers, judges, and others connected with the temple service.

3. To pay the rabbis for inspecting the sacrifices.

4. To furnish funds for building repair and water supply.

5. To provide for numerous other items, including women who wove or washed the temple linen.[27]

The tax was due in the spring of the year, and it was now fall.[28] Although the scriptures do not mention it, it seems logical to assume that Jesus had paid this tax in other years, especially those prior to his ministry.[29] But now he had revealed himself to be the Son of God; he who would pay a ransom for all need not pay the tax for the temple. It was his temple, and the offerings were made to him. The tax collectors' question concerned the basic relationship between the Lord and the Jewish rulers.

Peter, in answering the question, and in his zeal to protect the honor of his Master, pledged the payment. He then retreated to the house to converse with the Lord on the matter. Jesus, who could perceive the thoughts of all men, apparently knew his intent and, before Peter could speak, questioned him in the form of an allegorical teaching. The question was based on custom; kings assessed tribute and were paid—but by whom, their children or strangers? Peter answered that strangers paid the tributes. The Lord continued and asked if the children were not then free? The meaning was clear. The Son of God was free from the tax, but others were required to pay it. Once again it was affirmed to Peter who the Lord really was.

Jesus chose to avoid the potential conflict over this trivial matter and to support Peter. But the funds were not to come from the Apostles' treasury. Peter was to cast a hook into the lake; the first fish he caught would have lodged in its mouth sufficient money to cover the tax for both Jesus and Peter. Jesus instructed Peter to take that money and "give unto them for me and thee."

It is not recorded what the collectors did throughout this entire sequence. They may have waited outside while Peter went into the house to get the tribute. If that were the case, they would have seen Peter leave to go fishing. They might have watched as he threw his hook into the sea, caught the fish, and retrieved the coin from its mouth. If this were the case, it would be amusing to know their reaction.

An interesting distinction comes from the phrasing Jesus used when he agreed to pay the tax. He stated that the money should be used for "me and thee," and not "us." After his resurrection, Christ declared to Mary at the tomb that she should inform the Apostles that he was ascending "unto my Father, and your Father; and to my God, and your God" (see John 20:17). He was not as other men, even with his disciples.

Jesus used Peter's dilemma to teach a spiritual lesson, and the miracle sealed the teaching. Peter had created the problem in his overzealous desire to protect the Lord's honor. The Lord knew of his predicament even before Peter told him about it. Jesus was constantly aware of and concerned with every activity of his Apostles, whether he was with them physically or not.[30]

Part Eight

The Message
of the Miracles

The Message
of the Miracles

The miracles Jesus performed dramatically characterized his personality. They mirrored his love, his compassion, his kindness, and his personal concern for mankind. They taught and witnessed gospel principles and testified of the long-awaited Messiah.

The Gospels preserve but a glimpse of Jesus' life. To record all that he accomplished would require volumes. Through the Atonement, he took upon himself the sins of the world; through his miracles, "he hath borne our griefs" as well (Isaiah 53:4). The people came to him wherever he was. They brought their sick and afflicted of every kind, and with his boundless compassion he healed them all.

The individual miracles found in the Bible were recorded for specific reasons. They taught doctrine, witnessed Christ's divinity, and evidenced his love and concern for the smallest common problems. Christ witnessed his divinity to the people and to the rulers, and he appealed to their law. The people recognized the signs of the looked-for Messiah and remembered, but for the most part they would not accept Jesus in that role. The demons from the world of evil spirits recognized and obeyed him, but his chosen people would not. He openly claimed to be the Messiah, and performed miraculous feats to seal his testimony, but he was accused of doing it by the power of Beelzebub. The people loved their law more than they loved the Lawgiver. Isaiah accurately prophesied that the people of Christ's day would say, "we did esteem him stricken, smitten of God" (see Isaiah 53:4).

The Lord cast out evil spirits and caused the blind to see. He made the lame to walk and cured all manner of disease, both publicly and privately. Ultimately, he raised the dead as a specific witness to his power, majesty, and teaching. He healed by his word, in stages, by touch, and from a distance.

He caused the miraculous to become commonplace among the people, and he proved that he ruled the natural laws and the elements. He taught the Apostles of his great power, and assisted them as they developed their faith in him and in the authority he had given them. He forgave men's sins, both great and small. And even as they arrested him to kill him, he healed one more time, that he alone would suffer.

Christ healed the body so that the spirit could more freely believe. He offered temporal blessings in the hope that God's children might accept eternal blessings. Some were satisfied with only a temporal healing, but others saw through the facade of the flesh and glimpsed the spiritual meaning in all he did.

The message of the miracles is no different today than it was when Jesus delivered it. Some see, and want yet another sign; some accept immediate blessings that better only their temporal existence; but his sheep hear his voice, regardless of how he calls. In New Testament times the Lord's miracles produced hate, disbelief, anger, and rejection; they also produced faith, belief, hope, acceptance, and salvation. It is the same today with the miracles of Jesus the Messiah.

Notes

Introduction:

1. Farrar 2:9.
2. Ed. 1:478.
3. One additional miracle, the transportation by the Spirit of the Lord, is treated in note form only. By John's wording at the conclusion of his account of the miracle of walking on the water, I conclude he is mentioning this miracle briefly. See chapter 8, note 11.
4. Officially designated the Joseph Smith Translation (JST) in 1979. Formerly it would have been quoted as the Inspired Version of the Bible.
5. JC p. 149.

Chapter 1: Miracles

1. Ed 1:162—63. For a detailed listing of Old Testament passages Messianically applied with reference to rabbinical works see Ed 2:710—41.
2. Strauss p. 413.
3. Ed 1:162—63.
4. Ed 1:176.
5. See Ed 1:162—69 for a thorough treatment of the rabbinical expectations of the Messiah.
6. Farrar 1:170.
7. Trench p. 13.
8. JC p. 148—49.
9. MD p. 506.
10. Trench p. 50.
11. Geikie 2:6.
12. MM 3:28; Farrar 1:168.

Chapter 2: A Remembrance of Old Testament Events

1. Ed 1:227.
2. Ed 1:230.
3. Ed 1:163.
4. Ed 1:162—63.

5. This is the only mention of the city of Nain in the scriptures. There has been speculation on its location, but its exact location is of no particular importance to the miracle. For detail on this material see Trench pp. 258—59; Ed 1:552—53.

6. See Ed 1:554—57 for detail of the funeral and burial ceremony in existence among the Jews at the time of Christ.

7. Ed 1:557.

8. Josephus, Wars, Book II, I:3.

9. Josephus, Wars, Book VI, IX:3.

10. Ed 2:65.

11. Trench p. 289.

Chapter 3: Recognized by Demons, Accused by His Own

1. Ed 2:770—76; JC pp. 182—83.

2. Trench p. 171.

3. HC 2:503.

4. Ed 2:773—75.

5. MM 2:37; Geikie 2:4; Trench p. 162.

6. Ed 2:748—63.

7. Ed 1:478—79.

8. Farrar 1:455.

9. Ed 2:197.

10. JST Matthew 8:29 resolves this conflict, reporting only "a man."

11. It is generally agreed between the scholarly authorities that the Gospel writers were not describing an exact location but a general area. The scripture reports that after the miracle the herdsmen who witnessed it went into both city and country to report the event and the people then gathered to see the results.

Historically three cities have been identified with the general location, i.e., Gadara, Gerasa, and Gergesa. Gadara has generally been rejected because it was too far inland. Gerasa and Gergesa have both been identified with the ruins of Kersa, the location generally thought of as the site of the miracle. For further detail see; Ed 1:606—07; Farrar 1:333—34 and notes; JC p. 323, note 3; Trench pp. 162—64 and notes.

12. Trench p. 179.

13. Ed 1:607—8, Trench p. 179.

14. Trench p. 184—85.

15. TG, Outer Darkness.

16. MM 2:282.

Chapter 4: The Result of Verbal Claims

1. For detailed information on the synagogue at the time of Christ, its regulations, the conduct of those within, and the service itself, see Ed 1:430—50.

2. Under rabbinical law there were two corporal punishments (considered divine punishments) that could be inflicted upon individuals for religious violations. They were known as the "forty stripes save one," and the so-called "rebel's beating." The forty stripes save one was "inflicted after a regular judicial investigation and sentence, and for the breach of some negative precept or prohibition; while the . . . [rebel's beating] was, so to speak, in the hands of the people, who might administer it on the spot, and without trial, if any one were caught in supposed open defiance of some positive precept, whether of the law of Moses or of the traditions of the elders" [Ed(Temple) pp. 66—67]. The rebel's beating was usually to the death. Stephen was martyred in this manner (see Acts 7:57—58), and it was attempted upon Paul when he brought a Gentile beyond the designated limit in the temple: "and the people ran together: and they took Paul, and drew him out of the temple: . . . and . . . they went about to kill him" (Acts 21:30—31). Another time, Paul was stoned and left for dead (see Acts 14:19). The justification for this procedure supposedly came from the example of Phinehas, the son of Eleazar (see Num. 25:7—8). But the punishment inflicted upon Stephen and Paul (and attempted upon the Lord) was, in each case, contrary to all the rules of rabbinical criminal law [see Ed(Temple) pp. 65—68].

3. DNTC 1:462—64.

4. An interesting experience in the history of The Church of Jesus Christ of Latter-day Saints involving this miracle is recorded by Joseph Smith: "Towards the latter end of August [1830], in company with John and David Whitmer, and my brother Hyrum Smith, I visited the Church at Colesville, New York. Well knowing the determined hostility of our enemies in that quarter, and also knowing that it was our duty to visit the Church, we had called upon our Heavenly Father, in mighty prayer, that He would grant us an opportunity of meeting with them, that he would blind the eyes of our enemies, so that they would not know us, and that we might on this occasion return unmolested. Our prayers were not in vain, for when within a little distance of Mr. Knight's place, we encountered a large company at work upon the public road, amongst whom were several of our most bitter enemies. They looked earnest-at [sic] us, but not knowing us, we passed on without interruption. That evening we assembled the Church, and confirmed them, partook of the Sacrament, and held a happy meeting, having much reason to rejoice in the God of our salvation, and sing hosannas to His holy name. Next morning we set out on our return home, and although our enemies had offered a reward of five dollars to any one who would give them information of our arrival, yet did we get out of the neighborhood, without the least annoyance and arrived home in safety. Some few days afterwards, however, Newel Knight came to my place, and from him we learned that, very shortly after our departure, the mob came to know of our having been there, when they immediately collected together, and threatened the brethren, and very much annoyed them during all that day." (HC 1:108—9.)

Chapter 5: Miraculous Conclusions

1. For specific information on these materials, see Trench p. 268; Geikie 2:86–87.

2. JC p. 206.

3. Geikie 2:87–88.

4. A word used by later Jews to denote the cloud of brightness that symbolized God's divine presence. It was a symbol of God's special blessing of Israel. (See Ex. 24:16; 1 Kgs. 8:10; Isa. 6:1–3.) The symbol was further perpetuated in some New Testament occurrences. (See Matt. 17:5; Luke 2:9.)

5. Ed (Temple) pp. 61–62.

6. Farrar 1:374–75.

7. MM 2:48.

8. Trench pp. 217–18; Geikie 2:21–22. The house may have been a two-story home having on the second floor a larger room designed for meetings, or it may have been a single-story house with a covered courtyard. Both were common for the day.

9. Ed 1:505.

10. Geikie 2:23.

11. Ed 2:178.

12. Geikie 2:297–99.

13. Geikie 2:298.

14. Farrar 2:80.

15. Ed 2:178–79.

16. Ed 2:178.

17. Ed 2:180–81; MM 3:200–201.

18. MM 3:201.

Chapter 6: An Appeal to the Law

1. Ed 1:94.

2. Ed 1:93–108.

3. Geikie 2:24.

4. Geikie 2:99.

5. Ed 2:59–60.

6. Ed 2:56.

7. Geikie 2:24; Ed 2:777–87.

8. Ed 2:59–60.

9. Geikie 2:99.

10. MM 3:228.

11. Geikie 2:318.
12. MM 3:230.
13. MM 3:230.
14. Geikie 2:317.
15. JC p. 449.

Chapter 7: Selection and Call

1. JC p. 227.
2. Geikie 1:516–17.
3. MM 4:288.

Chapter 8: Signs and Powers

1. Strauss pp. 496–99; JC pp. 308–9.
2. MM 2:273–74.
3. MM 2:276; Ed 1:600.
4. Trench p. 154.
5. Trench p. 156.
6. MM 2:278.
7. Geikie 2:177.
8. JC p. 336.
9. JC p. 337.
10. JC p. 337.

11. John 6:21 contains what I have called the miracle of transportation by the Spirit of the Lord. Here John makes a very interesting addition to the miracle that was left unrecorded in the other Gospels. When Jesus came into the ship, the purpose and teaching of the miracle of walking on the water was over. At that point John records that they were "immediately . . . at the land whither they went." I take it this means they did not continue rowing or using sails to catch the wind, but were transported by the power of the Lord through the remaining distance. This I deduce and assume from the literal meaning of the word *immediately*.

There are other specific examples of this type of miracle. Philip, one of the seven called to assist the Apostles (see Acts 6:3–6), experienced such travel. He had completed his teaching of the eunuch and had baptized him. When he came "up out of the water, the Spirit of the Lord caught away Philip, that the eunuch saw him no more: . . . But Philip was found at Azotus," preaching. (Acts 8:39–40.) Philip traveled under the influence of the Spirit of the Lord, and the ordinary requirements of travel were not binding upon him.

Nephi, the son of Helaman, had a similar experience: "He was taken by the

Spirit and conveyed away out of the midst of them. And . . . he did go forth in the Spirit, from multitude to multitude, declaring the word of God," (Helaman 10:16–17.) The Spirit carried Nephi away to mountaintops (see 1 Nephi 11:1; 2 Nephi 4:25). Adam was baptized in such an experience (see Moses 6:64).

Additional examples of this miracle apparently are evident wherein prophets have been transported (frequently recorded as "in the spirit") to designated areas to receive visions from the Lord. (See Moses 1:1; Ezekiel 37:1; 2 Corinthians 12:2; Revelation 17:3; 21:10.)

Although such events are not described as separate and distinct miracles, it is obvious from the scriptures that this miraculous power has been used many times to further God's work.

12. Ed 2:55.

13. Trench p. 193.

14. Ed 1:619.

15. MM 2:289.

16. Nicodemus came to Jesus to ask questions of him (see John 3:1–7), but also defended Jesus before the officers of the Pharisees that would arrest him (see John 7:50–51). He also brought myrrh to anoint Christ's body after his death (see John 19:39).

17. Ed 2:374–75.

18. MM 3:346; Ed 2:375.

Chapter 9: A Gospel for All People

1. Geikie 2:105.

2. Ed 1:544.

3. MM 2:182–83; JC p. 251.

4. Ed 2:39.

5. Elder Bruce R. McConkie refers to the multitude as "Jews and Gentiles" (MM 3:17). Elder James E. Talmage refers to them as "semi-pagan" (JC p. 356). I refer to them as Gentile because of the arguments presented.

6. A single blessing on the food was distinctively Jewish (Ed 2:65).

Chapter 10: They Ask of Him a Sign

1. Ed 1:168–79.

2. Ed 1:167, 308–35.

3. Ed 2:275–77.

4. Ed 2:276–77.

5. Jesus did not personally go to the spirit prison, because those who were there could not abide his presence. But he opened the way so that others

from paradise might pass over and teach the gospel to those in the prison, who might then, through diligence, repentance, and the grace of God, extricate themselves from that awful condition.

6. MM 3:270.

7. Ed 2:317.

8. Geikie 2:315; Ed 1:238.

9. Ed 1:128.

10. Ed 2:556.

11. Ed 2:556.

12. Ed (Temple) p. 100.

Chapter 12: It Is I

1. JC p. 683.

2. MM 4:275.

3. JC p. 681.

4. JC p. 686.

Chapter 13: The Source of His Power

1. Ed 1:424.

2. Trench p. 128.

3. MM 2:11.

4. Ed 1:428.

5. Geikie 2:157.

6. Ed 1:620.

7. Ed 1:620, note 1.

8. Ed 1:622—26.

9. Ed 1:624.

10. Ed 1:624.

11. An interesting experience is recorded in Church history involving "virtue going out" of the Prophet Joseph Smith, as follows: "Elder Jedediah M. Grant enquired of me the cause of my turning pale and losing strength last night while blessing children. I told him that I saw that Lucifer would exert his influence to destroy the children that I was blessing, and I strove with all the faith and spirit that I had to seal upon them a blessing that would secure their lives upon the earth; and so much virtue went out of me into the children, that I became weak, from which I have not yet recovered; and I referred to the case of the woman touching the hem of the garment of Jesus. . . . The virtue here referred to is the spirit of life; and a man who exercises great faith in

administering to the sick, blessing little children, or confirming, is liable to become weakened." (HC 5:303.)

Chapter 14: A Kingdom for All People

1. Ed 1:491–96.
2. Geikie 2:13.
3. Trench p. 230–34.
4. MM 2:45.
5. Ed 1:495.
6. Ed 1:492.
7. Trench pp. 231–32.
8. Trench p. 230.
9. MM 2:45.
10. Trench p. 233.
11. Ed 1:492.
12. Geikie 2:13.
13. The raising of the daughter of Jairus, chapter 8; the two blind in the house, chapter 15; and healing one who was deaf and dumb, chapter 16.
14. Ed 1:492.
15. JC p. 471.
16. MM 3:285.
17. JC p. 471.
18. DNTC 1:537.

Chapter 15: That the Blind May See

1. Geikie 2:13.
2. Trench p. 212.
3. Trench p. 469.
4. Ed 2:49.
5. MM 2:297.
6. MM 2:298–99.

Chapter 16: Increasing Faith Through Miracles

1. Ed 2:44–45.
2. Ed 2:45.

3. Ed 2:46.

4. Ed 2:46.

5. MM 3:28—29.

6. Ed 2:47.

7. Ed 2:48.

8. MM 3:29.

Chapter 17: The Apostles Instructed in Faith Through Miracles

1. Some have speculated that Jesus still shone from the experience on the Mount of Transfiguration, but it is highly unlikely that Jesus would display such evidence of that special, spiritual experience and testimony before the multitude when he had reserved it solely for the three leading Apostles.

2. MM 3:72—73.

3. MM 3:73.

4. MM 3:74.

5. See also the healing of the Syrophenician woman, chapter 9; and the healing of one deaf and dumb, chapter 16.

Chapter 18: Resolving Personal Problems

1. "Israel is said to have been ten times called in Scripture 'bride' (six times in Canticles, three times in Isaiah, and once in Jeremiah)." Ed 1:353, note 2.

2. "The Biblical proofs adduced for attaching this benefit to a sage, a bridegroom, and a prince on entering on their new state, are certainly peculiar. In the case of a bridegroom it is based on the name of Esau's bride, Machalath, (Genesis 28:9), a name which is derived from the Rabbinic 'Machal,' to forgive." (Ed 1:353, note 1.) Edersheim's interpretation apparently comes from the fact that prior to the marriage she was called "Basemath" (see Genesis 36:3), but changed her name at the marriage, and was "forgiven."

3. A sacrament was that which was to be kept sacred, an outward spiritual sign. Ed 1:352.

4. Ed 1:352.

5. Farrar 1:162—63.

6. DNTC 1:136.

7. Geikie 1:450.

8. Geikie 1:450.

9. MM 1:452.

10. Farrar p. 163.

11. Of this salutation Edersheim states, "No one who either knows the use of the language, or remembers that, when commending her to John on the Cross, He used the same mode of expression, will imagine, that there was anything derogatory to her, or harsh on His part, in addressing her as 'woman' rather than 'mother.' " Ed 1:361.

12. Farrar p. 165.

13. Ed 1:361.

14. John's Gospel was written to the Jews. Obedient Jews would have such water pots in their homes. Purification was one of the main requirements of the rabbinical law. The water was used to wash or purify the hands, both before and after dinner, and was also used to purify the vessels used. Ed 1:357.

15. DNTC 1:137.

16. Ed 1:362, note 4.

17. Ed 1:363.

18. Strauss pp. 519–27.

19. "The wine was mixed with water, . . . Various vintages are mentioned: among them a red wine of Saron, and a black wine. Spiced wine was made with honey and pepper. Another mixture, . . . consisted of old wine, water, and balsam; yet another was 'wine of myrrh;' . . . [and] wine in which capers had been soaked. To these we should add wine spiced, either with pepper, or with absinthe; and what is described as vinegar, a cooling drink made either of grapes that had not ripened, or of the lees. Besides these, palm-wine was also in use. Also various foreign drinks . . . and Palestinian apple-cider." Ed 2:208.

"It was customary to provide at wedding feasts a sufficiency of wine, the pure though weak product of the local vineyards, which was the ordinary table beverage of the time." JC p. 144.

"Fruit of the vine (Matthew 26:29), a light, sweet wine (normally unfermented); eaten with bread it was one of the staple foods of the day." DNTC 1:136.

20. Ed 1:355.

21. Geikie 1:451.

22. Geikie 1:450–51.

23. Ed 1:485.

24. Ed 1:486.

25. Ed (Temple) pp. 70–72.

26. Farrar 2:42.

27. Geikie 2:249; Ed (Temple) pp. 74–75.

28. Ed 2:111–12.

29. Ed 2:113.

30. Geikie 2:250.

Subject Index

—A—

Abraham, Jews claim lineage from, 60; saw Christ's day, 60

Abraham's bosom, paradise, 147

Andrew, at feeding of five thousand, 32; call of, 101; forsakes all to follow Jesus, 103

Apostles, call reaffirmed, 104; call reserved for the Melchizedek Priesthood, 100; dispute with scribes, 198; effect of raising of Jairus's daughter on, 121; instructed to go into Galilee, 105; frightened at Jesus on water, 114; ordained by Jesus, 100; proved at feeding of five thousand, 31; reaction at feeding of four thousand, 136; trying to understand Jesus, 112

Ax, floats and swims, 114

—B—

Barnabus, 129

Barren Fig Tree, miracle of, 121; teachings of, 122

Bartimaeus, healed of blindness, 185

Beelzebub, Jesus accused of performing miracles by, 9, 45

Beelzebub Argument, 43—49; alternative belief to Christ's authority, 45; destroyed, 54; turned upon promulgators, 47

Belief, born of signs, 11

Bethany, home of Mary and Martha, 149

Bethesda, miracle at pool of, 63

Bible, discrepancies in, 1; King James Version used for this book, 1

Bier, Jesus touches, 27

Blasphemy, Jews accuse Jesus of, 60, 62

Blind, healing signified removal of spiritual darkness, 183; miracle at Jericho, 184; miracle of two in the house, 183; symbol of spiritual decay, 182

Blind at Bethsaida, miracle of, 193

"Bottomless pit," future habitation of evil spirits, 52

—C—

Caiaphas, prophesies of Christ's death, 153

Cana, water turned to wine at, 203

Capernaum, centurion's servant healed at, 128; demoniac in synagogue healed at, 39; Jesus teaches in, 17; nobleman's son healed at, 168; one with palsy healed at, 69

Centurion's servant, miracle of, 126

Chuza, 168

Cleopas, 162

Coin in the Mouth of the Fish, miracle of, 209

Compassion, miracles an example of Christ's, 17

Council in heaven, spirits present at, 36

—D—

Daughter of Syrophenician, miracle of, 131

Dead, defilement upon contact with, 27; Jesus raises three, 24

Demoniac at Capernaum, miracle of, 39

Demoniac that was Legion, miracle of, 49

Demons, evil spirits called, 37; influence on swine, 53; Jesus speaks to, 40; live in tombs, 51; physically abused hosts, 37; source of, 35; worship Jesus, 51

Diaspora, Law of Moses altered by, 85

Disease, connected with possession, 37; God's providence and, 79; normal consequence of life, 79; sin and, 73; sin of parents and, 78; sin of unborn and, 77

Dumb Lunatic Child, miracle of, 196

—E—

Elements, the Lord's power over, 111

Elijah, and Jesus rejected, 59; food miraculously provided by, 32; Jordan River parted by, 114; mantle falls to Elisha, 11; widow's son raised by, 25

man healed on, 66, 76; Jesus
deliberately broke Law of, 82; Jesus
heals woman with infirmity on, 91;
laws on health and sickness on, 86;
length of journey on, 17; observed
only in form, 88; used by rabbis for
social entertainment, 94

Sabbath Law, complexity of, 86, Jesus
confronts, 85; stronghold of Jewish
law, 86

Samaritan, 180

Sanhedrin, 152

Satan, conflicts with Jesus, 200; exploits
of, 36; Lucifer became, 36; possessed
were not servants of, 37

Sermons, Jesus claims Messiahship by,
58; precipitate anger of crowd, 58

Shunammite woman, 25

Shechinah, and visible presence of God,
65

Sidon, 59

Signs, enforced claim to Messiahship,
10; miracles are, 10, 84; requested by
leadership, 47

Siloam, pool at, 81

Sin, all evil is, 36; leprosy and, 174;
disbelief in miracles is, 20; disease
and, 73, 76; Jesus has power to
forgive, 72

Solomon's Porch, Jesus teaches in, 61

Son of David, title of Jesus, 185

Spirits, all mankind were, 35; Jesus
has conflict with evil, 200; source of
evil and wicked, 35; third part
followed Satan, 36

Stilling the Tempest, miracle of, 108

Superstition, about pool at Bethesda, 65

Swine, of demoniac miracle, 52

Synagogue, clothing nècessary for, 172;
Jesus claims Messiahship in, 58; ruler
upbraids Jesus in, 92

Synoptic Gospels, defined, 2

—T—

Talmud, blind considered dead in, 182;
prescribes healing methods, 171, 209

Temple, glory no longer existed, 65;
Jesus teaches in, 60, 76; symbol of
Israel's chosen position, 65; tax of,
210

Thomas, 150

—U—

Unbelief, of mourners for daughter of
Jairus, 120

Urim and Thummim, 65

Uzziah, 176

—V—

Virtue, goes out of Jesus, 19, 173

—W—

Walking on Water, miracle of, 112

Water Changed to Wine, miracle of,
202

Widow's Son, miracle of, 23

Wine, drunk by Jesus, 206; Jewish
parable on, 207; made from water,
202

Woman with Infirmity, miracle of, 91

Woman with Issue of Blood, miracle of,
170

—Z—

Zephaniah, 183

Scripture Index

OLD TESTAMENT:

NEW TESTAMENT

THE PEARL OF GREAT PRICE

THE BOOK OF MORMON

DOCTRINE & COVENANTS